Origami Orig

By Robin Glynn

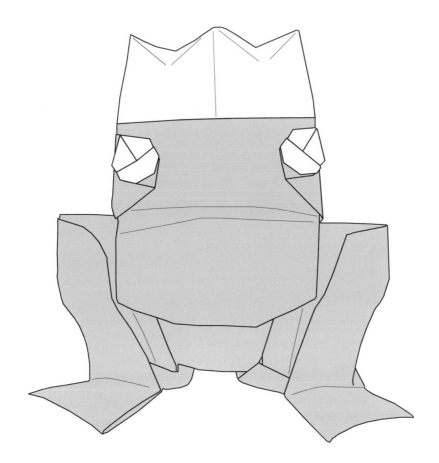

A collection of 47 original models

Thanks to all those who's ears I have bent

This book was written entirely by Robin Glynn,
so it's all my fault.

Introduction

My name is Robin Glynn and I have been interested in origami since I was 6 years old. At the time of writing this, that was 48 years ago. This is my first origami book, and at one book every 48 years, it will probably be my last.

Origami is such a wonderful pastime, it requires the minimum of materials and is rewarding in so many ways. It can be educational, therapeutic, stress reducing, challenging, practical and artistic.

I have divided this book into 4 sections - boxes, living things, objects, and decorations. Within each section I have ordered the models from easiest to most complex. None of the models are what I would call "super complex", but this book should not be regarded as a tutorial. If you are new to origami, you may wish to supplement this book with something that offers more guidance.

This introduction is deliberately short, as I am a man of few words and I am sure you would rather be folding that reading this stuff.

I hope that you enjoy this book, and have many more origami adventures.

Symbols and basic folding techniques

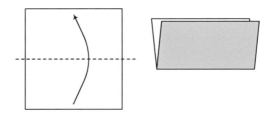

In Origami there are only two basic folds,
a dashed line indicates a valley fold...

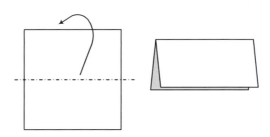

...and a line of dots and dashes indicates a
mountain fold. All other folds in Origami
are simply combinations of valley and
mountain folds

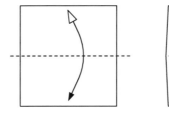

If the arrow is pointed at both ends it
means fold then unfold leaving a
crease

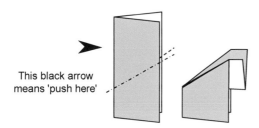

This black arrow
means 'push here'

This is an inside reverse fold. It sometimes
helps to make the crease first and then push
the paper where the black arrow indicates

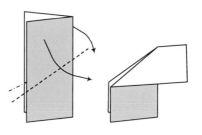

The outside reverse fold is a little more
difficult. Open out the paper and turn
the top half inside out

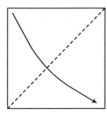

Next, lets try a squash fold. To show how to do this we need to do a few basic folds in preparation

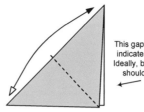

This gap is exaggerated to indicate the layer behind. Ideally, both front and back should match exactly.

Valley fold then unfold to make a crease

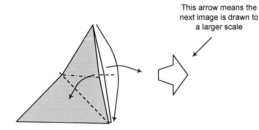

This arrow means the next image is drawn to a larger scale

Press the top point down while separating the two layers...

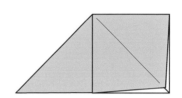

...and you have performed a squash fold

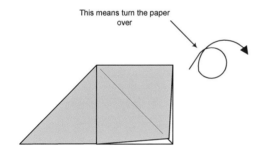

This means turn the paper over

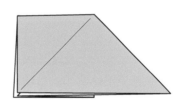

We shall continue folding this example to explain some more advanced procedures

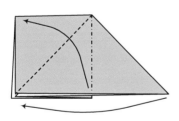

Make another squash fold

This symbol means rotate the model 45 degrees anticlockwise

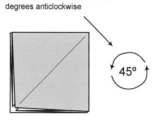

45°

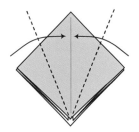

Fold the edges to the centre -
do not fold all the layers

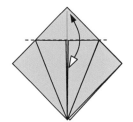

Fold and unfold

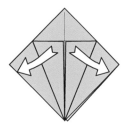

Unfold

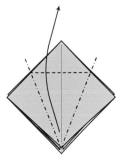

Lift a single layer and stretch it
up as far as it will go

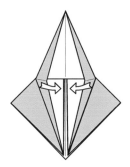

Allow the sides to come
together by reinforcing
the existing creases

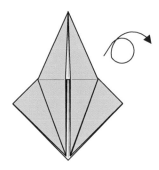

This is a petal fold

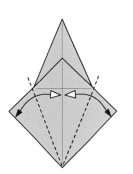

Petal fold

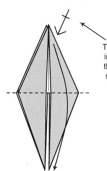

This is a bird base

This is a repeat symbol -
in this case fold the flap
that is at the back in the
same way as shown at
the front

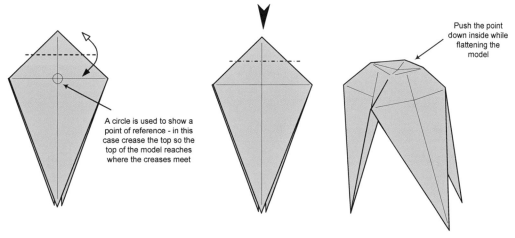

A circle is used to show a point of reference - in this case crease the top so the top of the model reaches where the creases meet

Push the point down inside while flattening the model

This move is a sink - where a point is reversed inside the model - it is a lot easier if you partially unfold the model

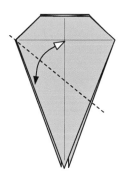

Crease - this is in preparation for a move call a "rabbit's ear"

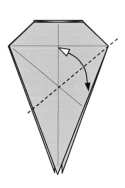

Another crease

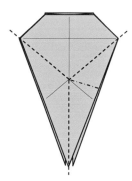

Now for the rabbit ear - pinch the sides of the point together

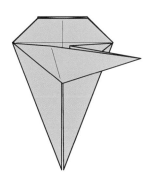

Flatten to finish the move

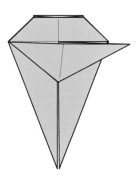

Rabbit ear complete

There are some other less common moves you may encounter. The best way to understand an unfamiliar procedure is to examine the next diagram and work out how to get your model to look the same. This book is not aimed specifically at beginners, but with a little perseverance, or in this modern age, a little Google search, I am sure you will get there. Good luck and happy folding.

Gift box
(p 12)

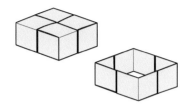

6 Sheet modular box
(p 15)

A4 modular box
(p 18)

9 Sheet hexagonal box
(p 21)

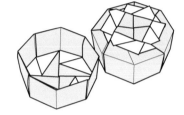

Octagonal modular box
(p 26)

A4 gift box
(p 29)

Business card holder
(p 32)

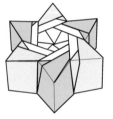

Star box
(p 36)

A5 Star box
(p 41)

Octagonal Star box
(p 46)

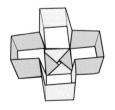

X Box
(p 52)

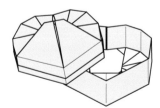

Heart Box
(p 56)

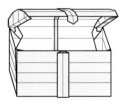

Treasure chest
(p 64)

Model index - Living things

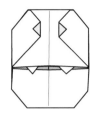

Pureland Dracula
(p 69)

The Grim Reaper
(p 72)

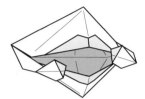

Greed
(p 77)

Teddy Bear
(p 82)

Cat
(p 86)

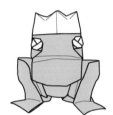

The Frog Prince
(p 90)

Monkey head
(p 94)

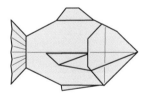

Fish
(p 98)

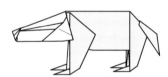

Badger
(p 104)

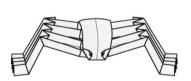

Spider
(p 109)

Monkey
(p 114)

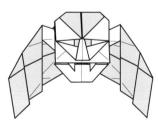

Dracula
(p 120)

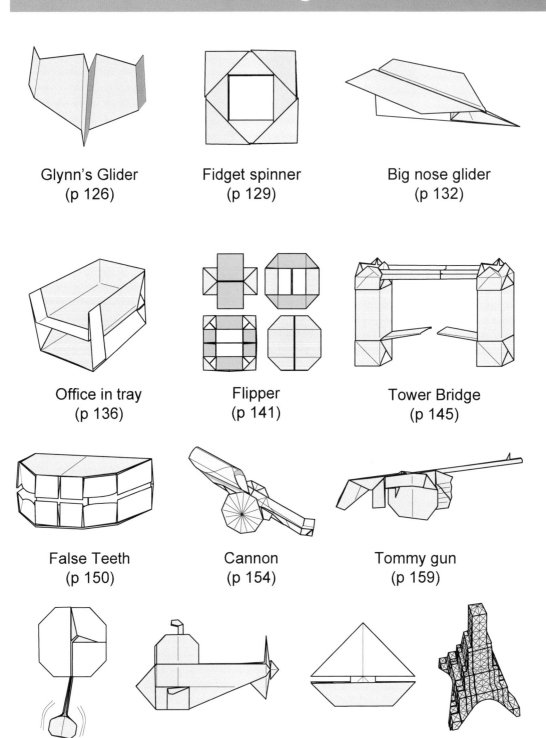

Glynn's Glider
(p 126)

Fidget spinner
(p 129)

Big nose glider
(p 132)

Office in tray
(p 136)

Flipper
(p 141)

Tower Bridge
(p 145)

False Teeth
(p 150)

Cannon
(p 154)

Tommy gun
(p 159)

Tick tock clock
(p 165)

Submarine
(p 170)

Yacht
(p 175)

Eiffel Tower
(p 181)

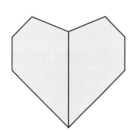

Heart Badge
(p 187)

8 Pointed Star
(p 190)

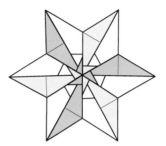

6 Pointed modular star
(p 193)

12 Pointed star ring
(p 196)

8 Pointed Woven Stars
(p 199)

6 Pointed Woven Stars
(p 203)

Braided Bird Star
(p 207)

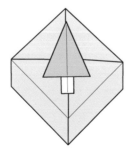

Xmas Tree
Box Decoration
(p 211)

Heart
Box Decoration
(p 214)

Gift Box

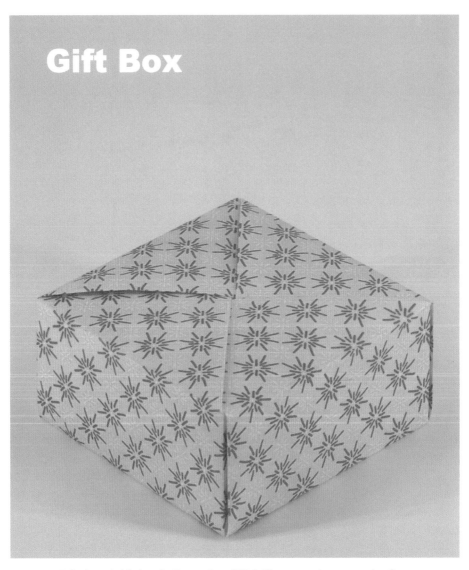

I designed this box in December 1999. However, I was not the first to arrive at this design. I found out later that the great Tomoko Fuse had designed this box some time before I did. It is often difficult to establish if a model is entirely original. This box is such a neat and logical solution, that it may well be that numerous origami enthusiasts have independently arrived at this design.

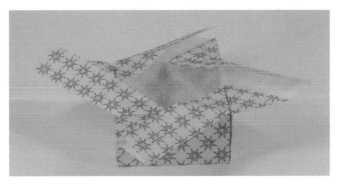

Gift Box

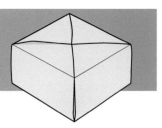

1

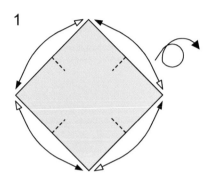

Pinch the half way points

2

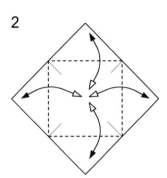

Fold the corners to the middle using the pinch marks as a guide

3

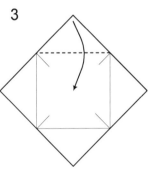

4

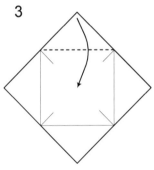

Using the circled areas as a guide valley fold the bottom corner up to the top edge

5

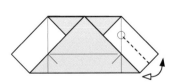

Crease only as far as the circled reference

6

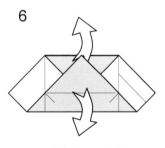

Unfold completely

7

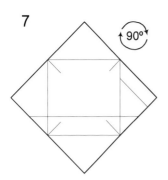

Rotate the paper ¼ turn.

8

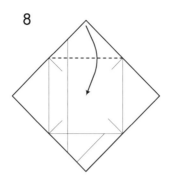

Repeat steps 3-7 on the
other 3 corners

9

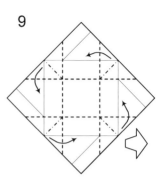

Begin to form a box

10

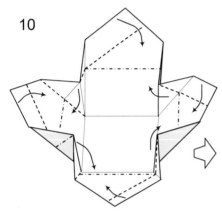

Continue to collapse the box,
incorporating the creases from step 5

11

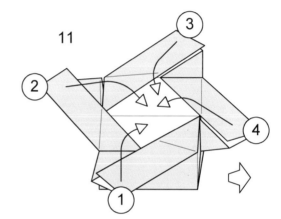

Finished box. Close by folding each flap
to the middle in the order shown.

11

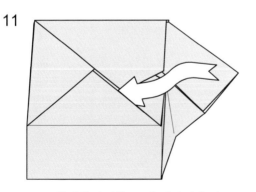

Tuck the last flap under to lock the box

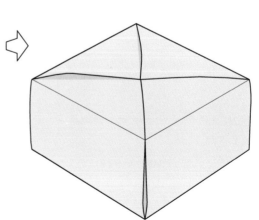

6 Sheet Modular Box

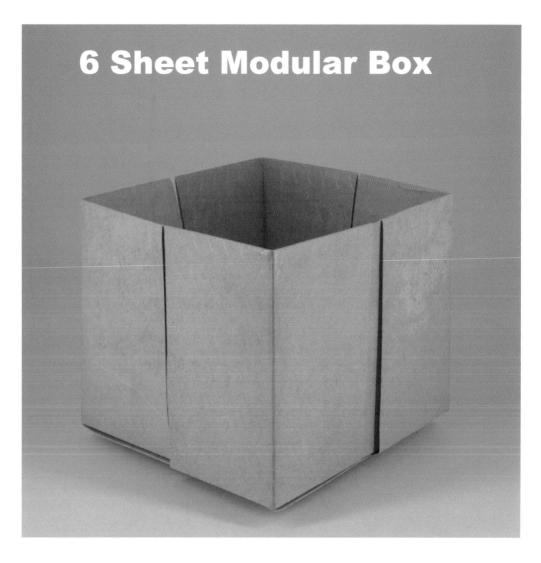

This box, designed in May 2017, can be made using rectangles with a wide variety of dimensions. The box pictured here is made using 3 A4 sheets of card cut in half vertically. This makes them approximately 3x1. If you use 2x1 rectangles, you get a much more shallow box. I have not seen this method used before, and it does have some advantages. It is simple to make and the sides can flex a little, so 2 identically sized boxes will fit together.

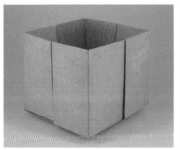  

6 Sheet Modular Box

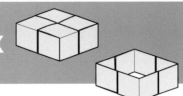

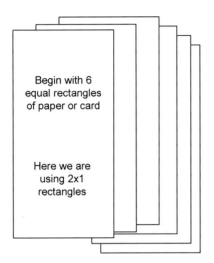

Begin with 6 equal rectangles of paper or card

Here we are using 2x1 rectangles

The width of the rectangle dictates how tall the box will be...

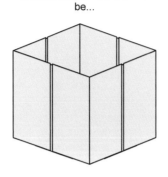

For a cube, use 3x1 rectangles

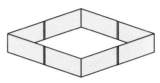

"A" sized paper makes a shallow box

1

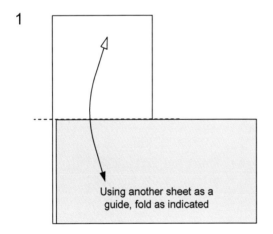

Using another sheet as a guide, fold as indicated

2

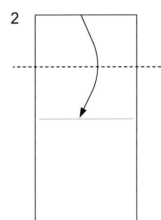

3

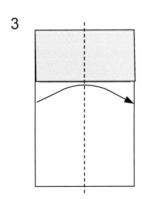

4

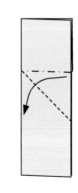

Fold the top layer only

Make 4 of these

Base

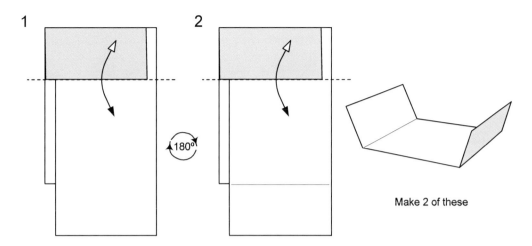

For the base of the box, use step 2 as a guide to make 2 creases

Make 2 of these

Assembly

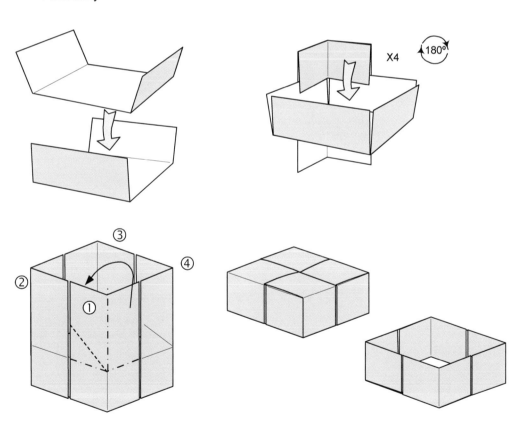

A4 Modular Box

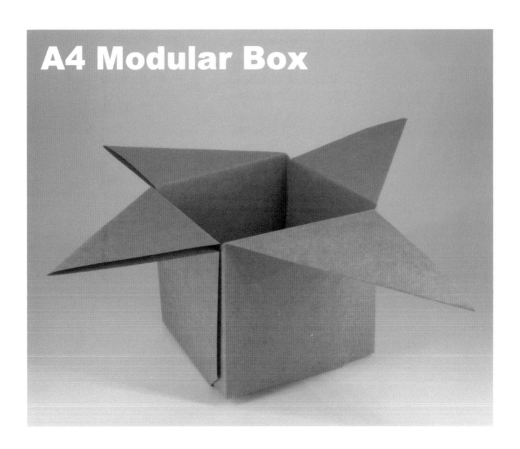

This box was designed in December 2008. The construction is very minimalist, but it holds together nicely and the double layered base makes it quite strong. It works well as a box for gifts - A4 card makes a perfect box for mugs.

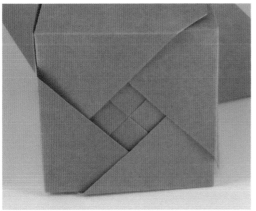

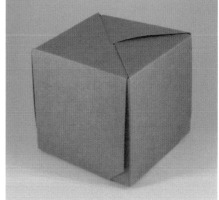

A4 Modular Box

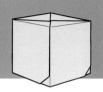

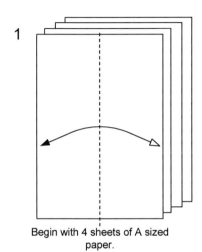

Begin with 4 sheets of A sized paper.

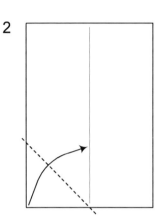

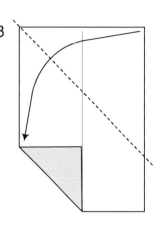

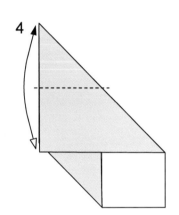

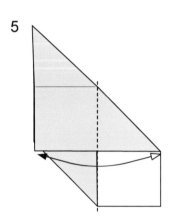

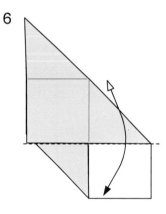

Mountain crease.

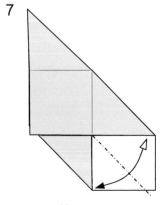

Fold on existing creases to make 3D.

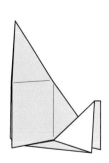

Finished unit, make 3 more

Assembly

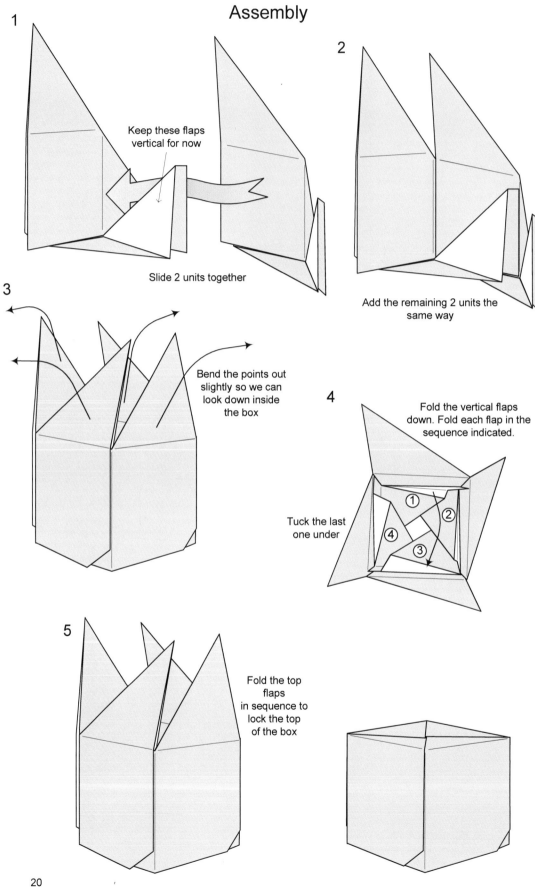

1 Keep these flaps vertical for now

Slide 2 units together

2 Add the remaining 2 units the same way

3 Bend the points out slightly so we can look down inside the box

4 Fold the vertical flaps down. Fold each flap in the sequence indicated.

Tuck the last one under

① ② ③ ④

5 Fold the top flaps in sequence to lock the top of the box

9 Sheet Hexagonal Box

Designed in May 2017. This was a natural progression of the 6 Sheet modular box. The diagram for this model includes a variation, but I prefer this version.

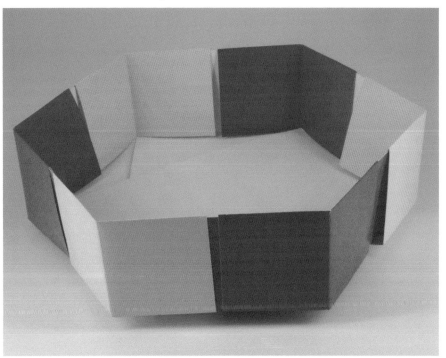

9 Sheet Hexagonal Box

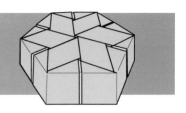

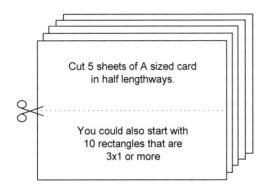

Cut 5 sheets of A sized card in half lengthways.

You could also start with 10 rectangles that are 3x1 or more

1

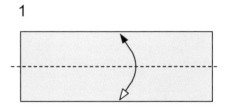

First we need a template

2

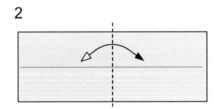

3

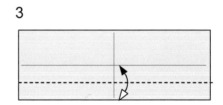

4

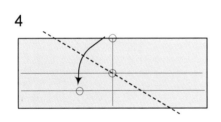

5

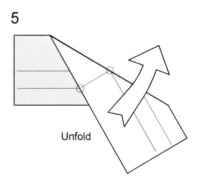

Unfold

6

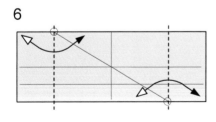

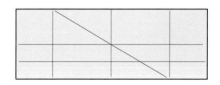

Template complete

Base

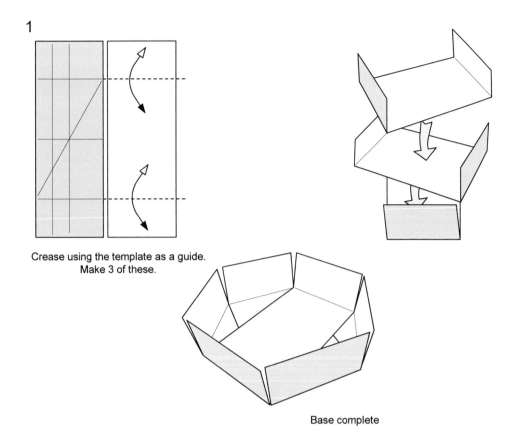

1

Crease using the template as a guide.
Make 3 of these.

Base complete

Sides

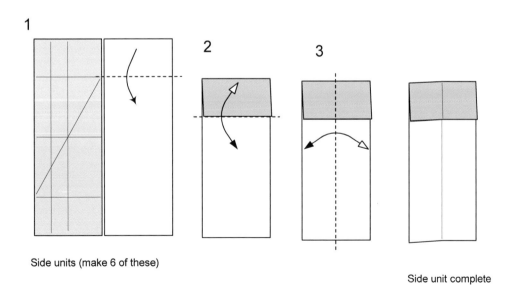

1

2

3

Side units (make 6 of these)

Side unit complete

Assembly

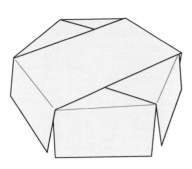

To begin assembly, arrange the
base units like this

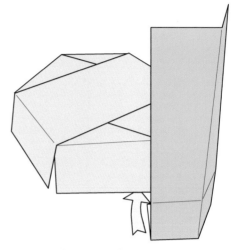

Slide each of the 6 units
into place

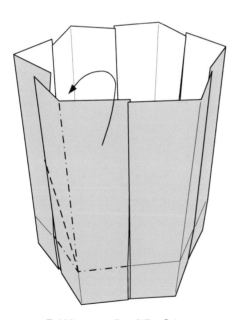

Rabbit ear a unit so it lies flat

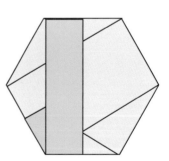

Viewed from above, the unit
should look like this

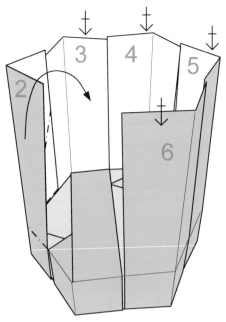

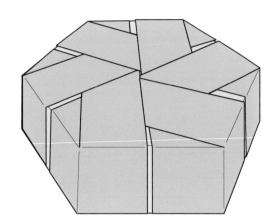

Repeat for the other 5 units, tucking the
last few tabs under

Variation

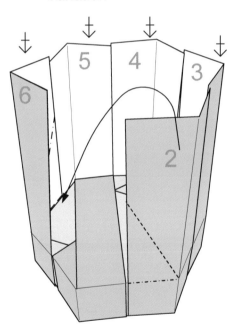

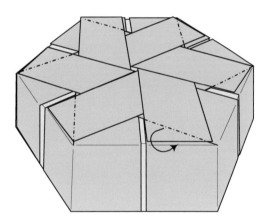

...you can mountain fold the ends
to lock the units

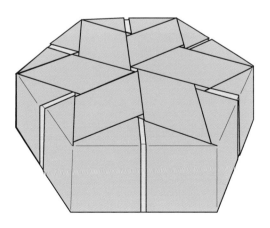

If you fold so that the end of each flap is
exposed...

Octagonal Modular Box

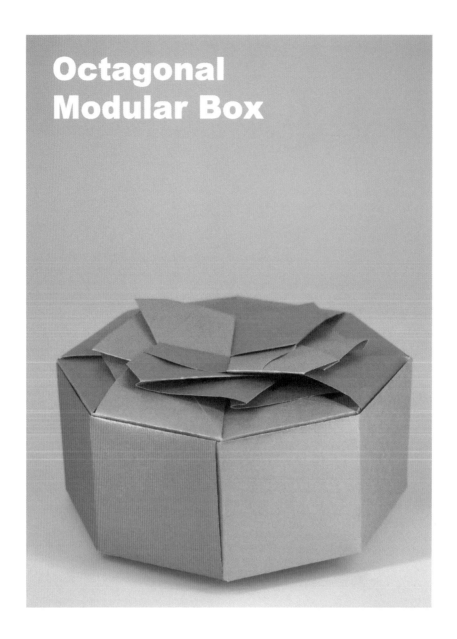

I designed this box in July 2017. It is such an obvious design, I am sure that others have also arrived at the same solution. There is just enough movement between the units, that they fit inside each other without having to make different sized boxes. It can be made with paper or thin card. This one is from some pearlised paper I bought from a car boot sale.

Octagonal modular box

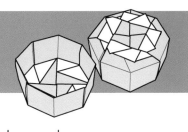

Start with 4 A sized rectangles

1

Divide into thirds

2

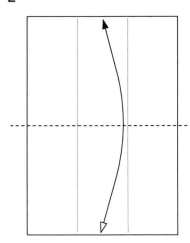

3

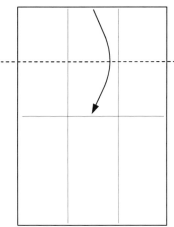

4

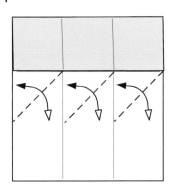

5

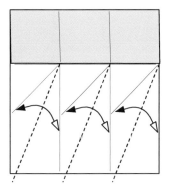

6

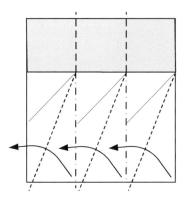

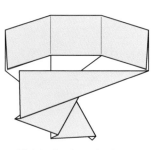

Finished unit, make 3 more.

Assembly

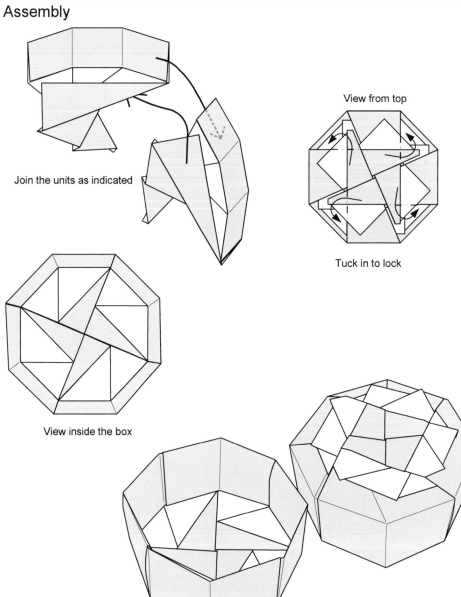

Join the units as indicated

View from top

Tuck in to lock

View inside the box

A4 Gift Box

This single sheet box was designed in September 2008. The folding
sequence makes no unnecessary creases and uses the geometry of
A sized rectangles to create a box with a square base.

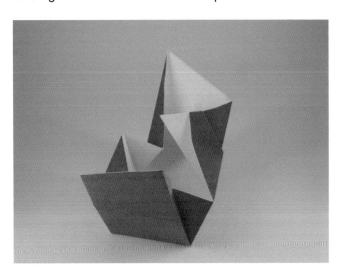

A4 Gift box

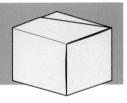

Begin with a sheet of A sized paper

1

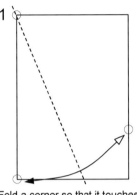

Fold a corner so that it touches the opposite edge

2

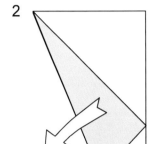

Unfold

3

4

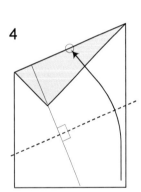

5

Unfold everything

6

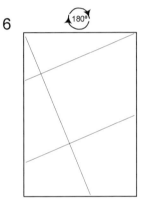

7

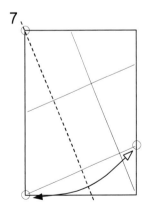

Repeat steps 1 - 5

8

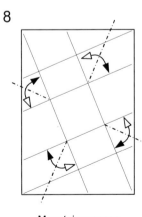

Mountain creases

9

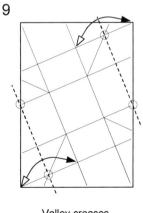

Valley creases

30

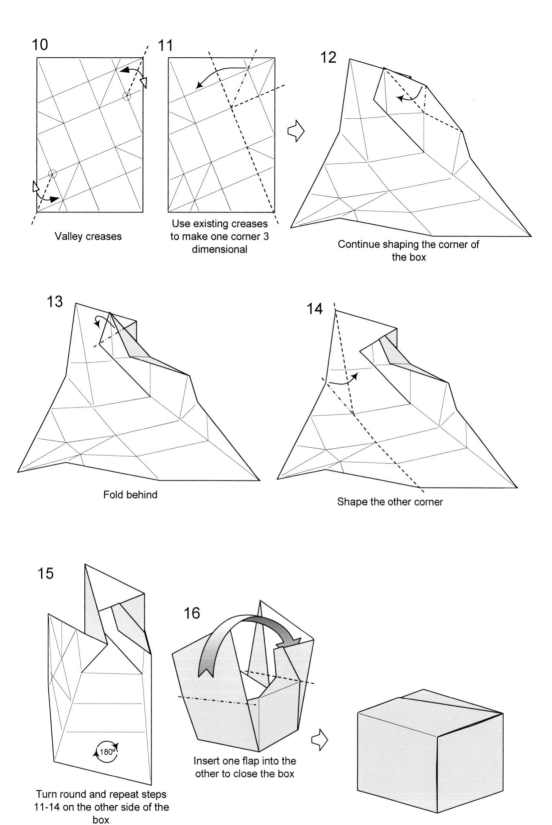

10

Valley creases

11

Use existing creases to make one corner 3 dimensional

12

Continue shaping the corner of the box

13

Fold behind

14

Shape the other corner

15

180°

Turn round and repeat steps 11-14 on the other side of the box

16

Insert one flap into the other to close the box

Business card holder

I designed this in March 2006, one year after starting my consultancy business. It is easy to fold, and works best using thick paper or card. With this, you are one step closer to becomming a millionaire!

Business Card Holder

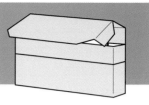

1

1/3
1/3
1/3

Begin with a sheet of A5. This will make a box suitable for standard 55mm x 85mm business cards

2

Make a small pinch

3

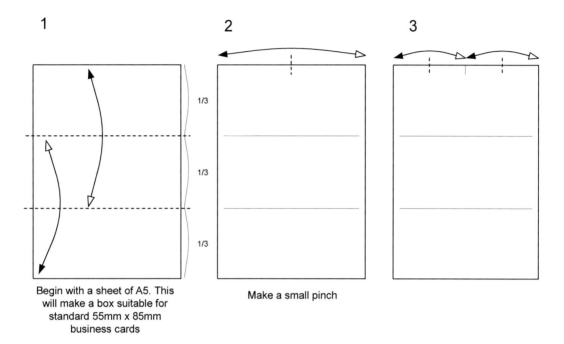

4

5

6

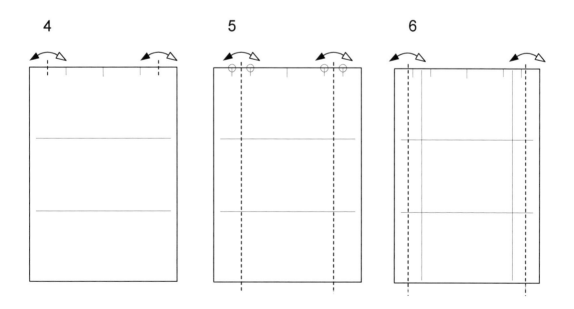

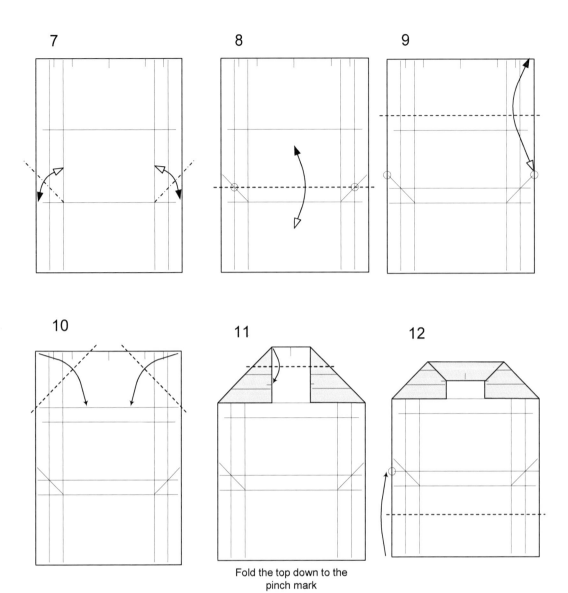

7

8

9

10

11

Fold the top down to the
pinch mark

12

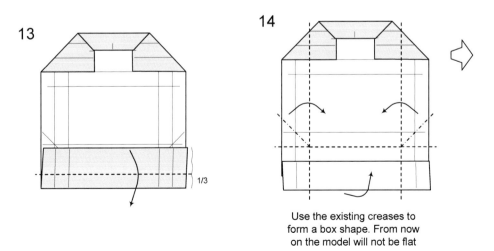

13

1/3

14

Use the existing creases to
form a box shape. From now
on the model will not be flat

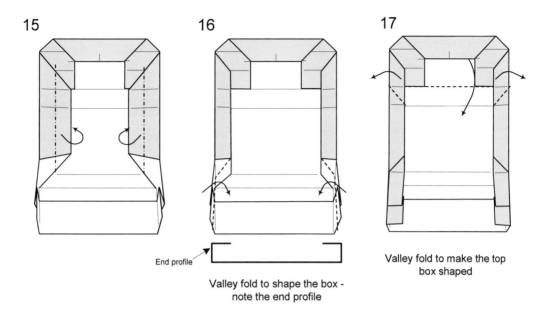

15

16

End profile

Valley fold to shape the box -
note the end profile

17

Valley fold to make the top
box shaped

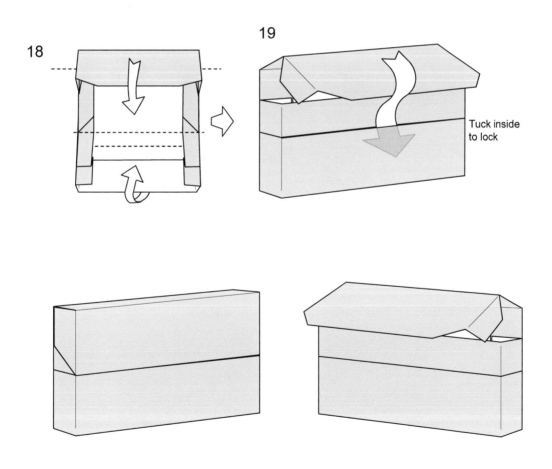

18

19

Tuck inside
to lock

Star Box

This is a new version of a model I originally designed in July 1998. I used to have a separate design for the lid, but star shaped boxes flex enough for this to not be necessary. It fits together really well, although I prefer to cheat and use bulldog clips to hold things in place during assembly.

Star Box

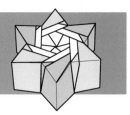

1
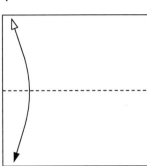

2
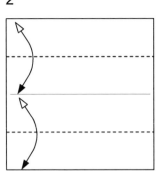

3
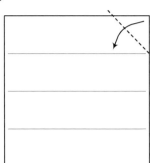

4
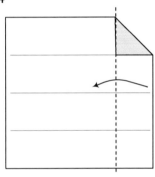

5
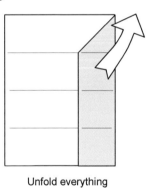

Unfold everything

6
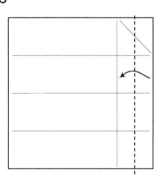

7
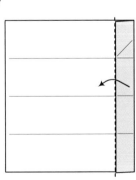

8
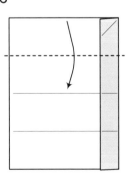

9
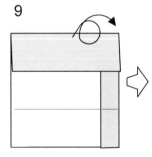

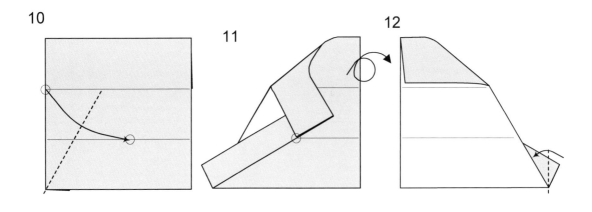

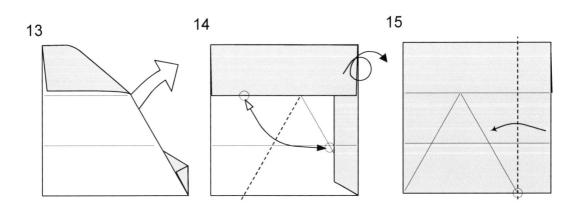

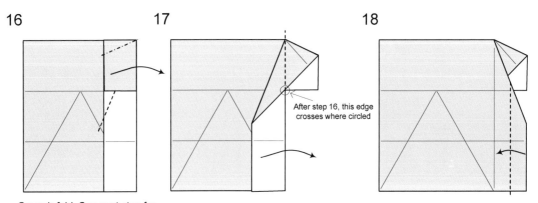

Squash fold. See next step for
exact position of diagonal crease.

After step 16, this edge
crosses where circled

19

20

21

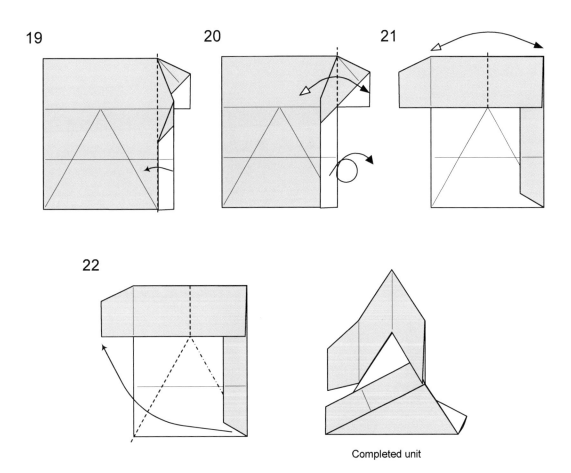

22

Completed unit

Assembly

1

To assemble,
mountain fold
the tab into
the pocket

2

Slide up

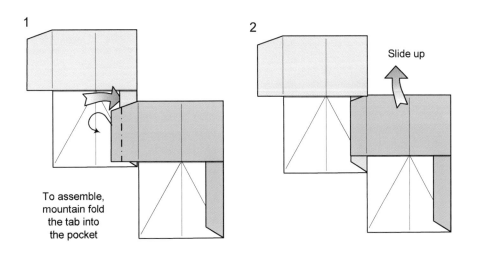

3

You don't have to do this, but bulldog clips can help keep things together at this stage

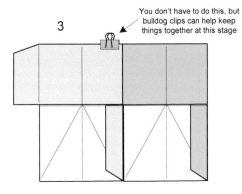

Join all 6 together

4

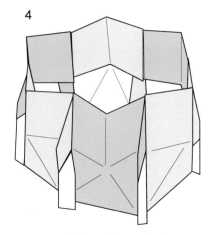

Re-fold step 22 on all units

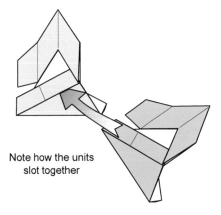

Note how the units slot together

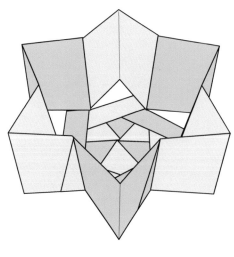

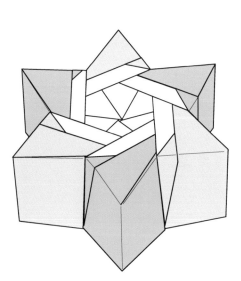

A5 Star Box

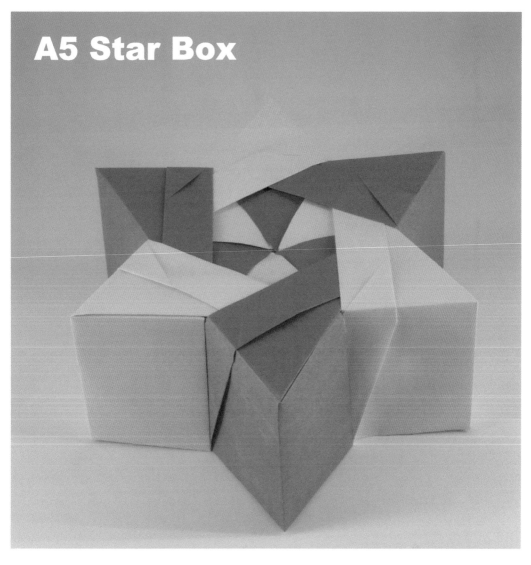

This model was designed in June 2017. "A" sized paper makes a
satisfyingly tall box, but it can be folded using almost any
rectangle. The assembly can be tricky, but when complete the box
is very strong.

 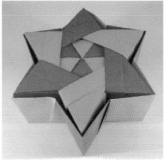 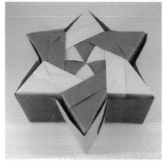

A5 Star Box

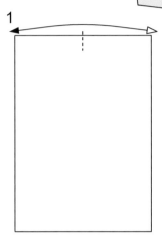

Begin with 6 rectangular sheets, these
diagrams show A sized paper

1

Make a small pinch

2

You can also pinch
here if it is difficult to
make an accurate fold

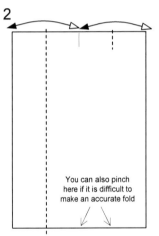

3

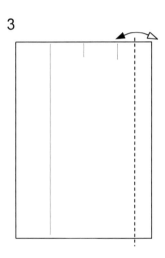

4

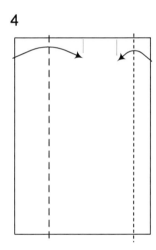

5

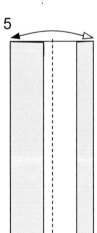

6

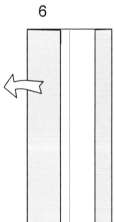

7

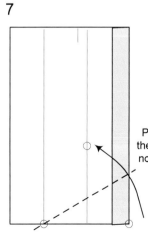

Place the corner on
the centre line, but try
not to make a crease

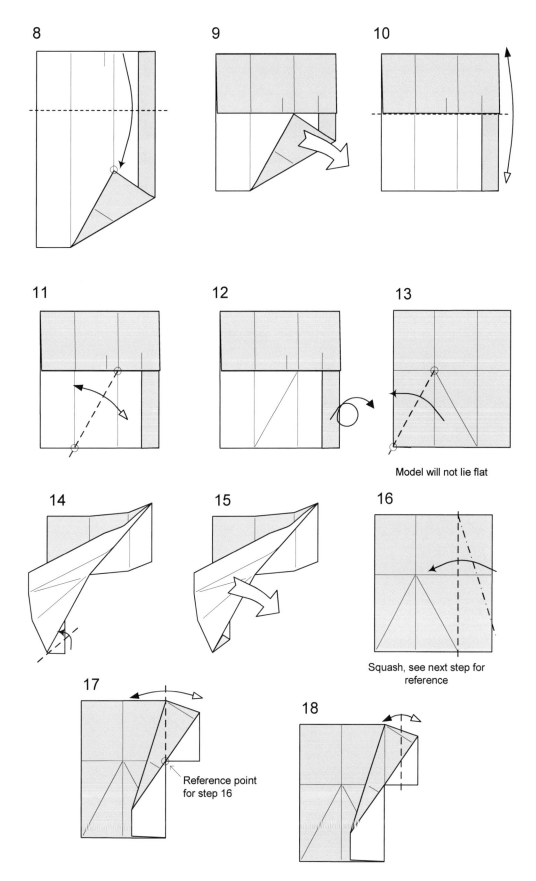

8

9

10

11

12

13

Model will not lie flat

14

15

16

Squash, see next step for reference

17

Reference point for step 16

18

19

20

21

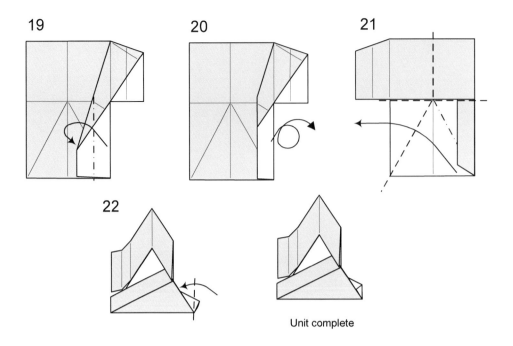

22

Unit complete

Assembly

1

To assemble,
mountain fold
the tab into
the pocket

2

Slide up

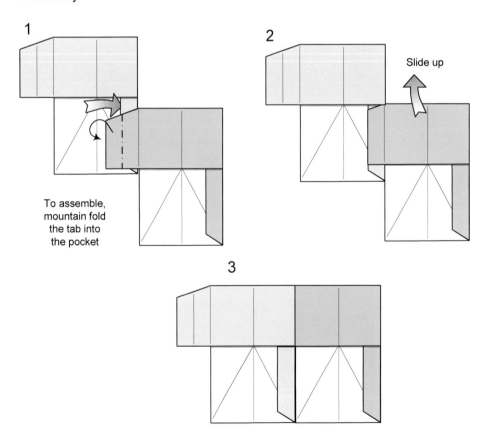

3

Join all 6 together

4

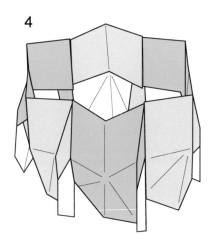

Re-fold the units
(see step 21)

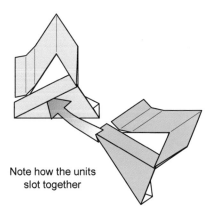

Note how the units
slot together

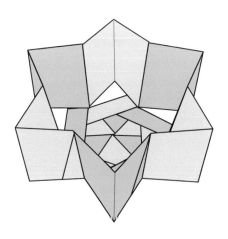

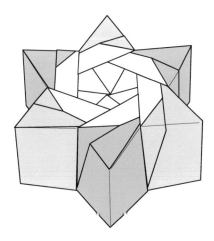

Octagonal Star Box

This box has been through a few versions. I settled on this design in January 2018. Earlier versions had too many layers in some places and was prone to tearing with thicker paper or card. I am much happier with this design. The model in the photographs is folded from A5 cartridge paper.

Octagonal Star box

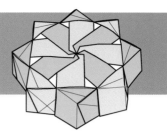

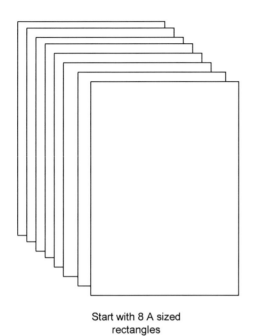

Start with 8 A sized
rectangles

1

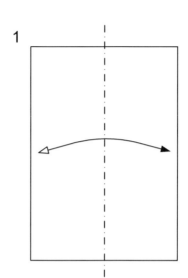

2

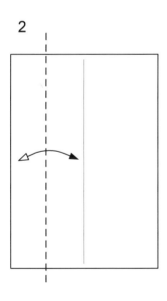

3

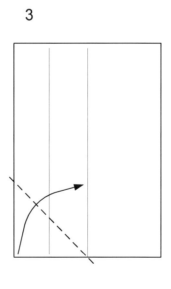

4

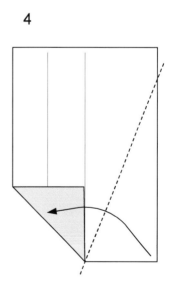

5

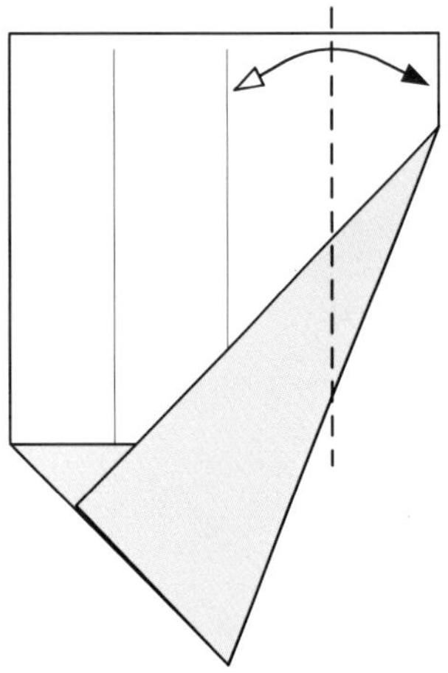

6

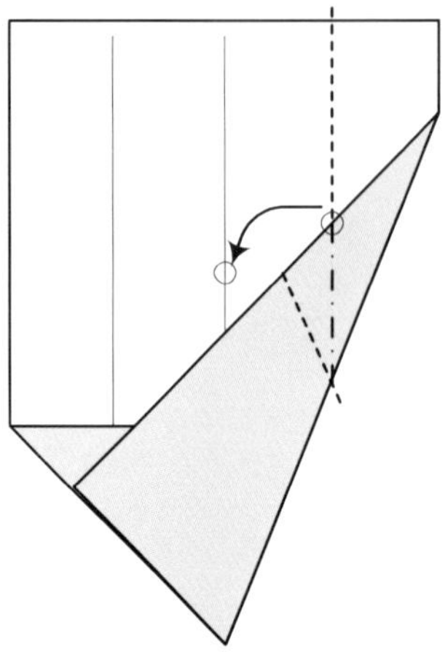

Squash fold

7

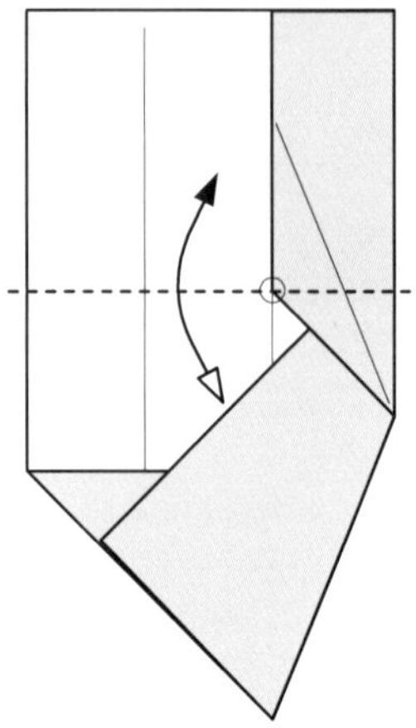

8

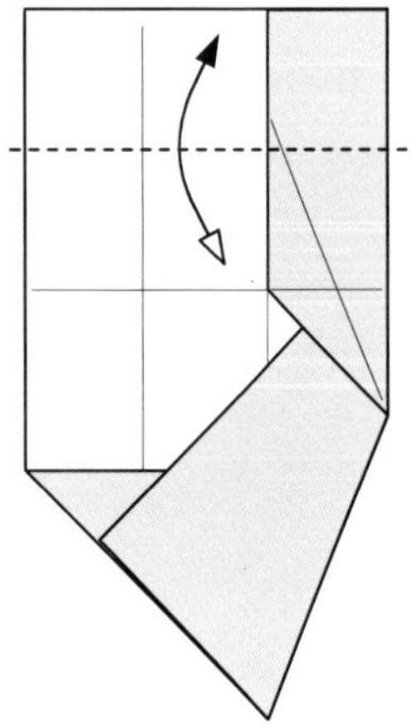

9

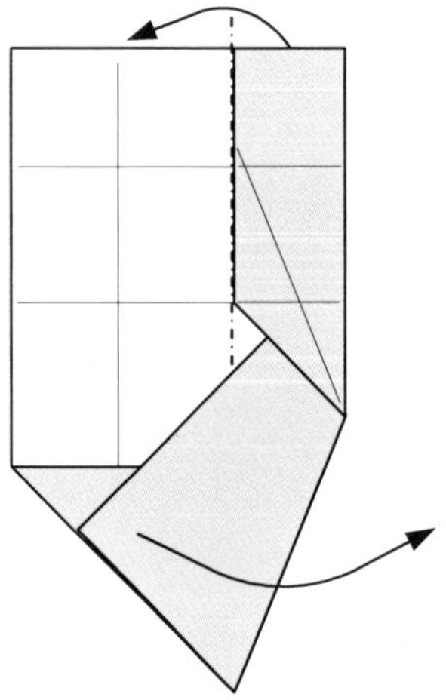

10

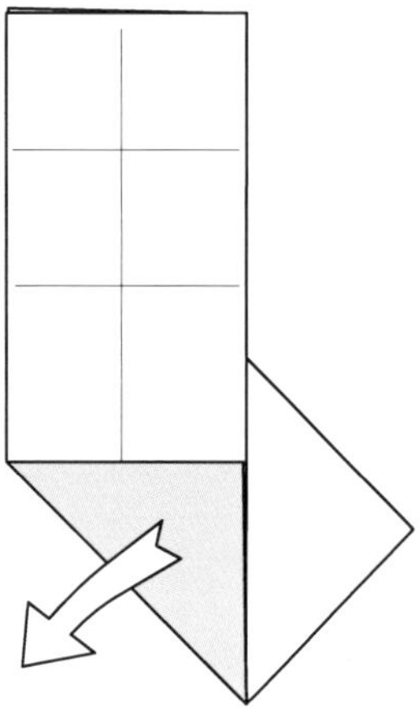

11

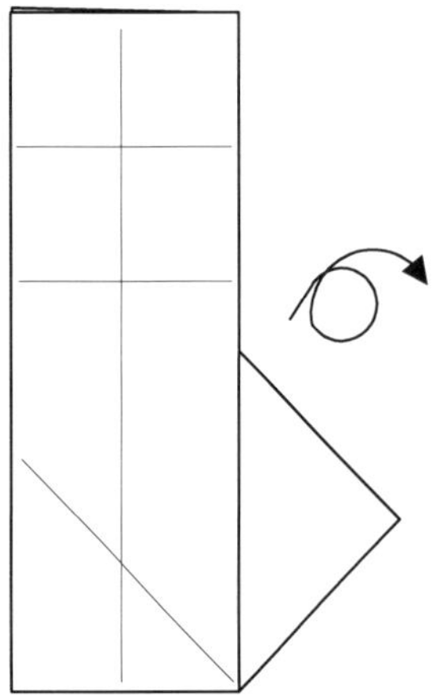

12

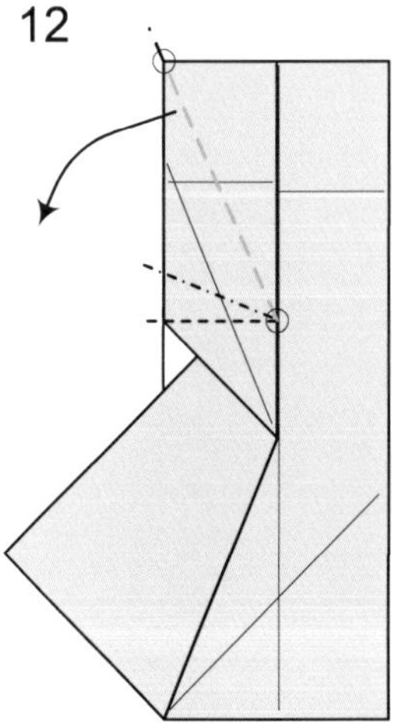

Squash fold

13

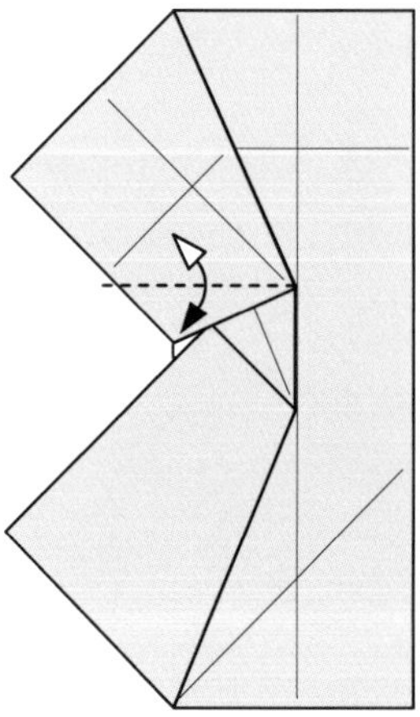

48

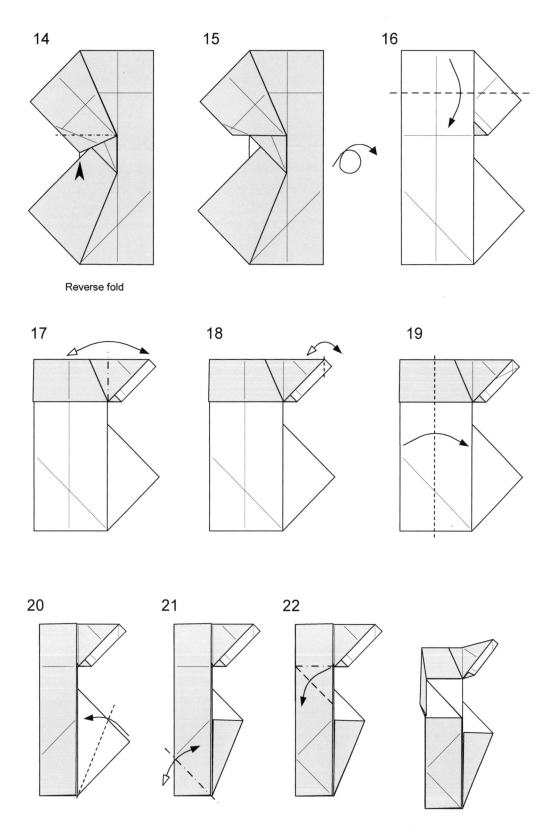

14

15

16

Reverse fold

17

18

19

20

21

22

Finished unit

Assembly

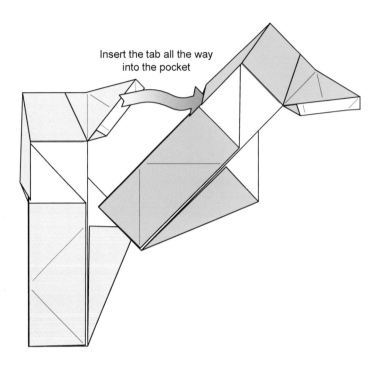

Insert the tab all the way into the pocket

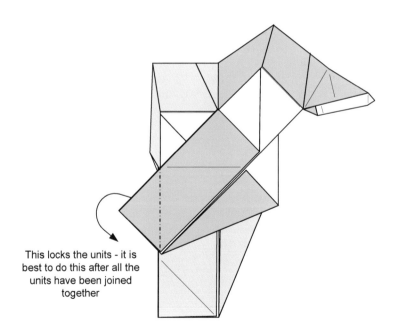

This locks the units - it is best to do this after all the units have been joined together

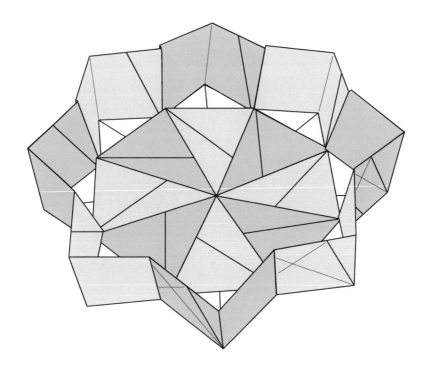

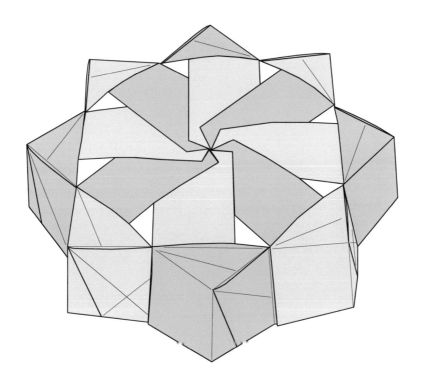

X Box

I designed this in July 2017. It took quite a few attempts to arrive at this design, but I am rather pleased with it. A taller box can be made if you start with rectangular paper. This shape has enough flexibility for the lid to fit without adjusting the size of the paper.

Box + lid = 8 bits

X Box

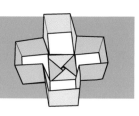

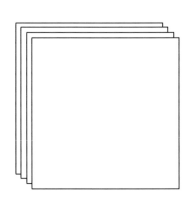

Begin with 4 squares

1

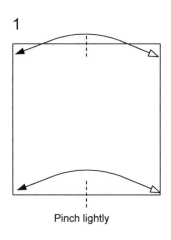

Pinch lightly

2

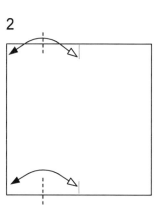

3

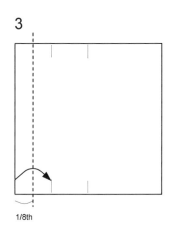

1/8th

4

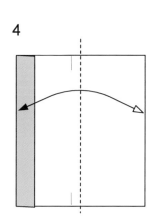

5

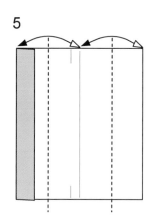

6

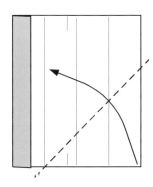

7

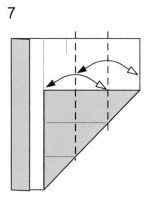

8

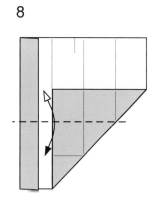

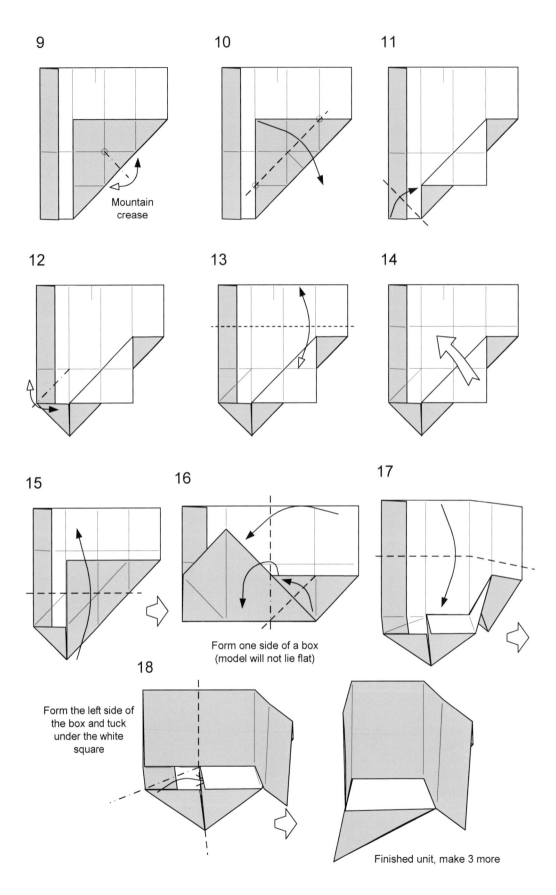

9

10

11

Mountain
crease

12

13

14

15

16

Form one side of a box
(model will not lie flat)

17

18

Form the left side of
the box and tuck
under the white
square

Finished unit, make 3 more

Assembly

1

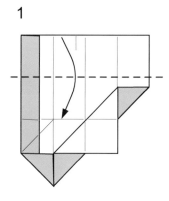

Unfold all units back to step 14

2

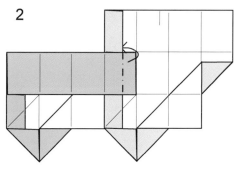

Mountain fold the tab into the pocket
then separate the 2 units

3

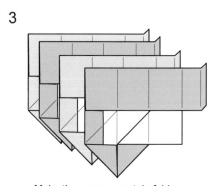

Make the same mountain fold
in all 4 of the units

4

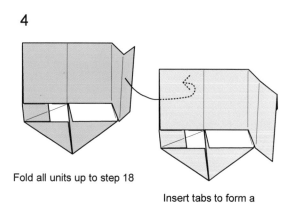

Fold all units up to step 18

Insert tabs to form a
loose box

5

Now re-fold step 18 on each unit

Tuck each point into its neighbour

Heart Box

This box was designed in March 2001. The model photographed here is folded from a roll of wallpaper I bought years ago from Poundland. The heart is a technically challenging shape for an origami box. Any box shape with an internal angle greater than 180° breaks the usual rules - so hearts crosses and stars (all included in this book) are less common in origami.

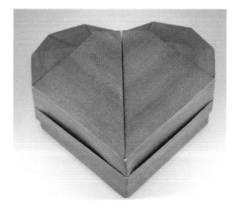

Heart Box

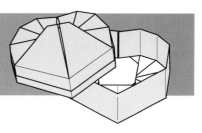

1

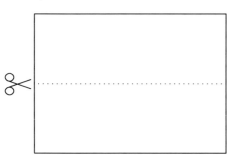

Cut a sheet of A4 in half lengthways

2

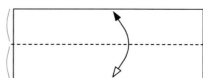

Keep the other half for the lid

3

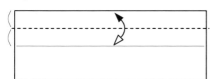

4

5

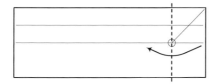

6

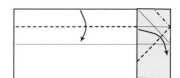

Squash fold

6b

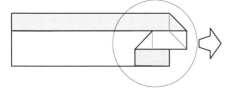

7

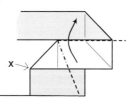

Squash fold so that 'X' lies along the
horizontal edge....

7b

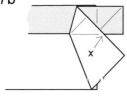

....Like this

8

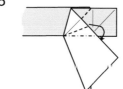

Swivel some paper behind

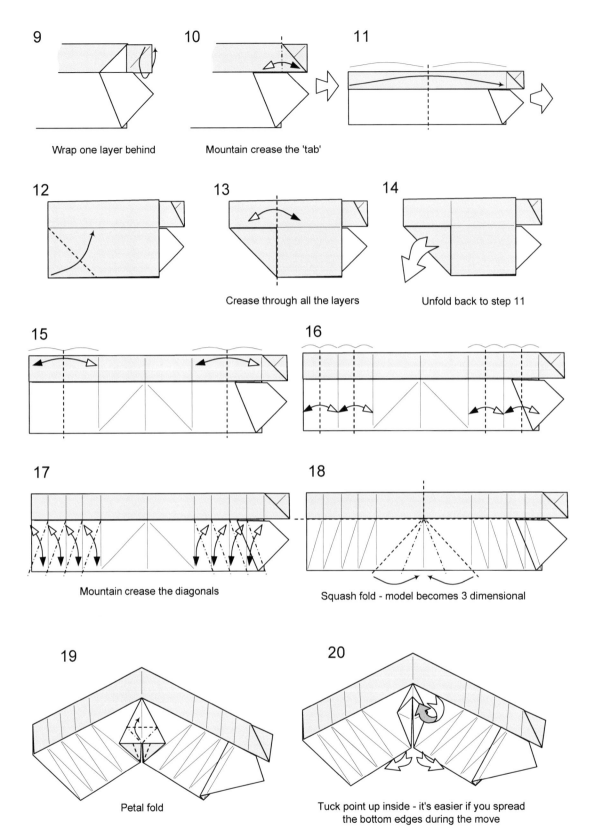

9

Wrap one layer behind

10

Mountain crease the 'tab'

11

12

13

Crease through all the layers

14

Unfold back to step 11

15

16

17

Mountain crease the diagonals

18

Squash fold - model becomes 3 dimensional

19

Petal fold

20

Tuck point up inside - it's easier if you spread
the bottom edges during the move

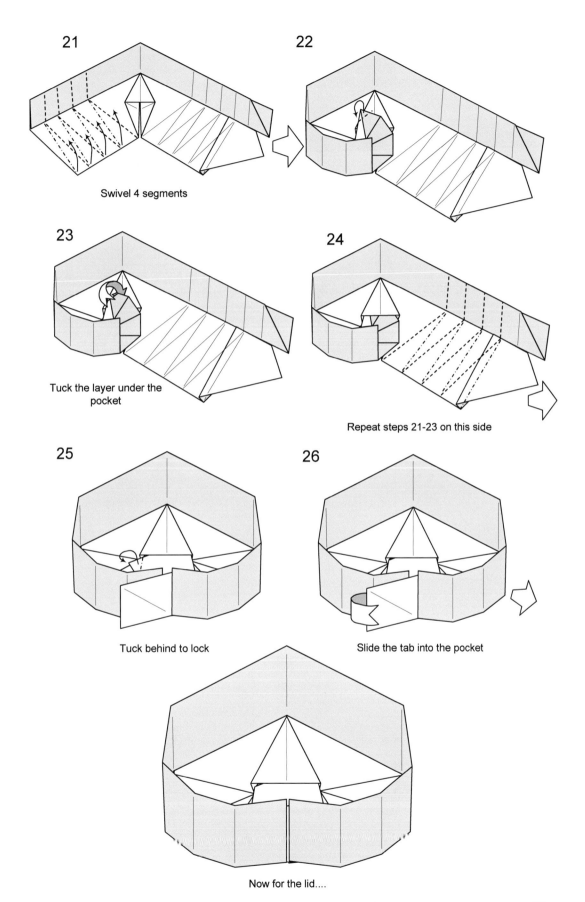

21

Swivel 4 segments

22

23

Tuck the layer under the pocket

24

Repeat steps 21-23 on this side

25

Tuck behind to lock

26

Slide the tab into the pocket

Now for the lid....

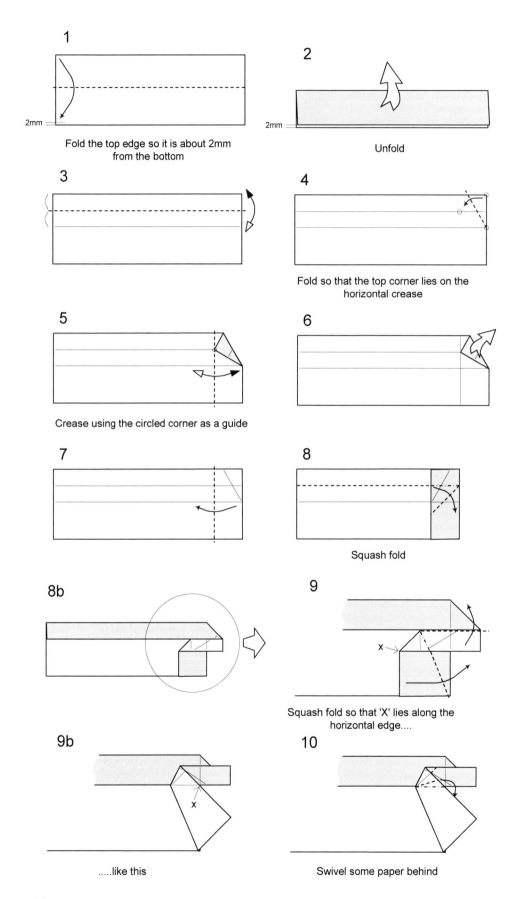

1

2mm

Fold the top edge so it is about 2mm
from the bottom

2

2mm

Unfold

3

4

Fold so that the top corner lies on the
horizontal crease

5

Crease using the circled corner as a guide

6

7

8

Squash fold

8b

9

Squash fold so that 'X' lies along the
horizontal edge....

9b

.....like this

10

Swivel some paper behind

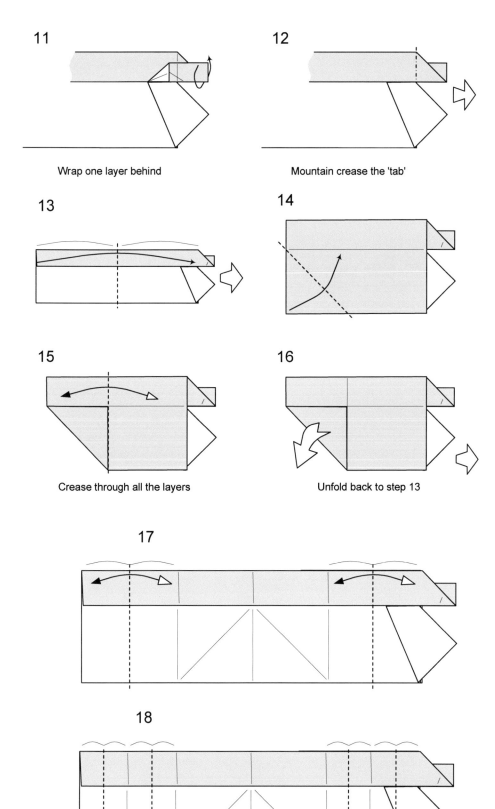

11

Wrap one layer behind

12

Mountain crease the 'tab'

13

14

15

Crease through all the layers

16

Unfold back to step 13

17

18

19

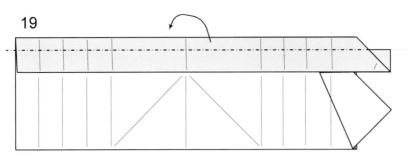

Mountain fold using the tab as a guide

20

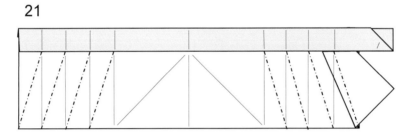

Reinforce as valley folds

21

Mountain crease the diagonals

22

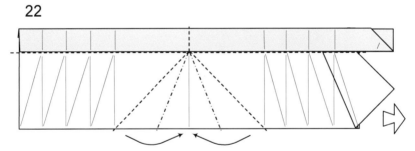

Squash fold - model becomes 3 dimensional

23

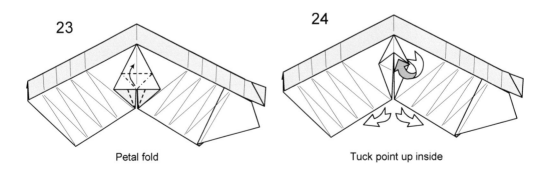

Petal fold

24

Tuck point up inside

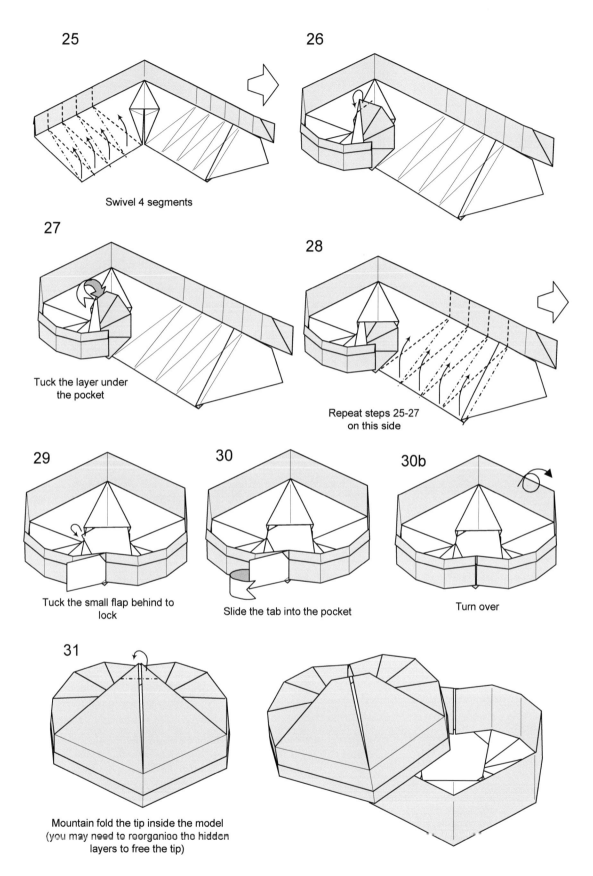

25

Swivel 4 segments

26

27

Tuck the layer under
the pocket

28

Repeat steps 25-27
on this side

29

Tuck the small flap behind to
lock

30

Slide the tab into the pocket

30b

Turn over

31

Mountain fold the tip inside the model
(you may need to reorganise the hidden
layers to free the tip)

Treasure Chest

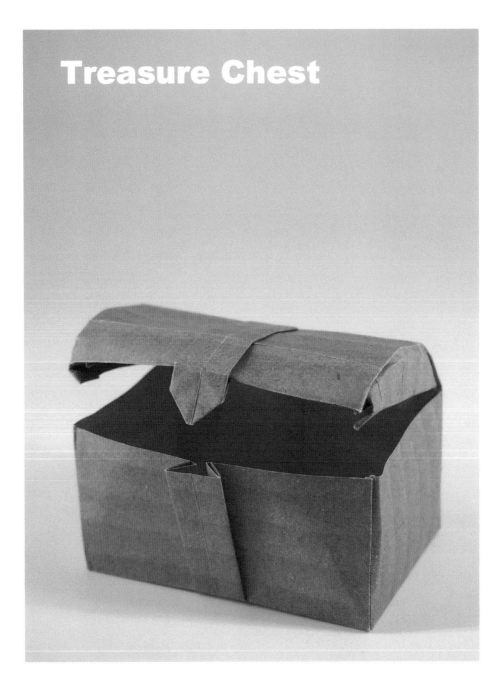

This model was designed in November 1997. It is not too challenging to make, but it does require a lot of care to make a neat and tidy model. If you can get hold of wood effect paper, it makes the model that much nicer. This one is folded from 20cm origami paper.

Treasure Chest

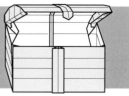

1

2

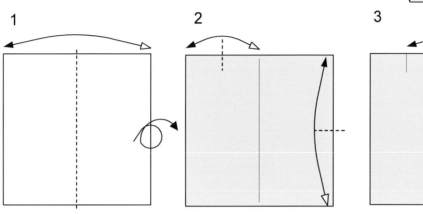

3

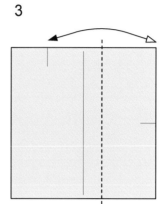

4

5

6

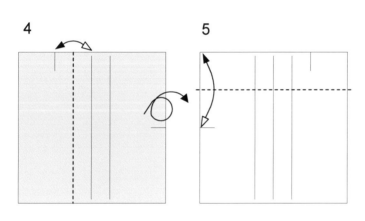

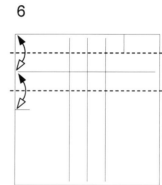

7

8

9

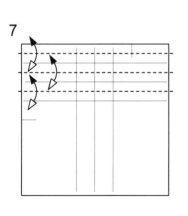

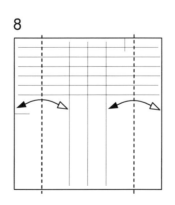

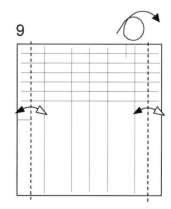

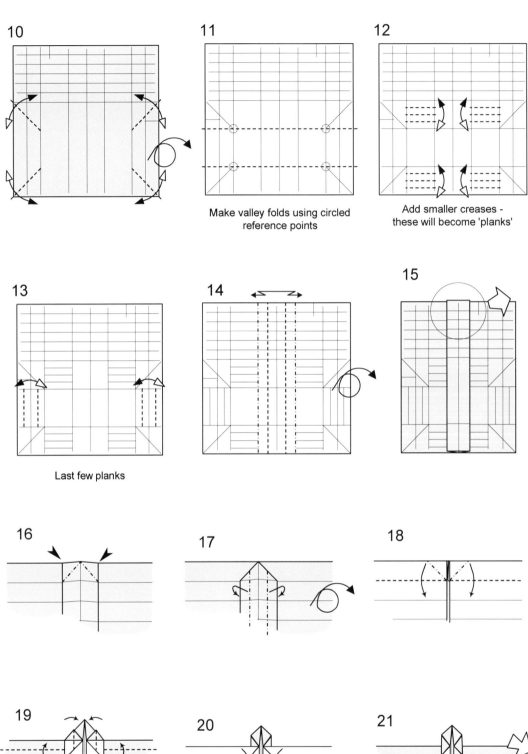

10

11

Make valley folds using circled
reference points

12

Add smaller creases -
these will become 'planks'

13

Last few planks

14

15

16

17

18

19

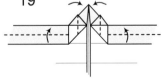

Swivel fold the edges

20

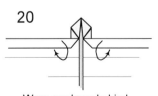

Wrap one layer behind
(colour change)

21

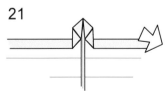

22

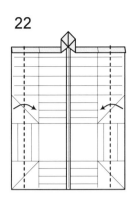

23

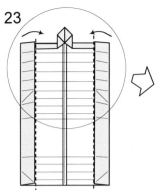

Fold the sides to make the
model 3D

24

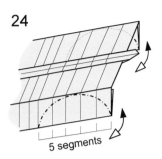

5 segments

Pinch a curved mountain crease
through both layers

25

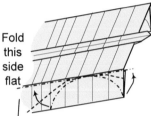

Fold
this
side
flat

Form a valley fold so that the curved
mountain crease lies on the straight
crease above it

26

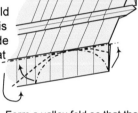

Next step viewed
from here

27

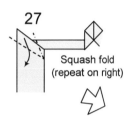

Squash fold
(repeat on right)

28

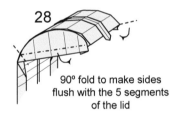

90° fold to make sides
flush with the 5 segments
of the lid

29

Unfold back to
step 22

30

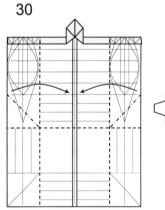

31

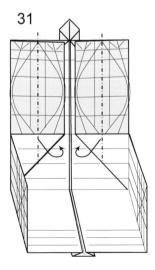

32

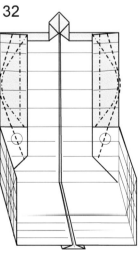

Reform the lid
(steps 24 to 29)
extending creases
at circled points

33

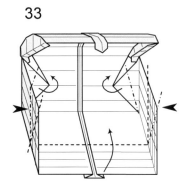

Tuck rear flaps behind to lock lid folds.
Form the front of the chest using existing creases.

34

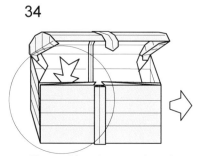

The next few steps are viewed
from inside the box

35

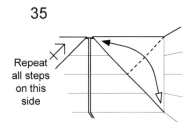

Repeat
all steps
on this
side

36

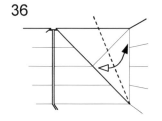

37

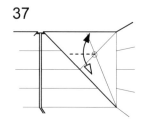

38

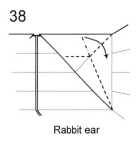

Rabbit ear

39

40

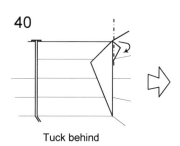

Tuck behind

41

Mountain crease tab

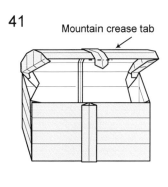

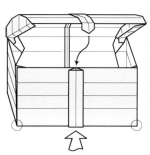

To lock, hold
circled corners
and gently push
the middle of
the base while
inserting tab

Pureland Dracula

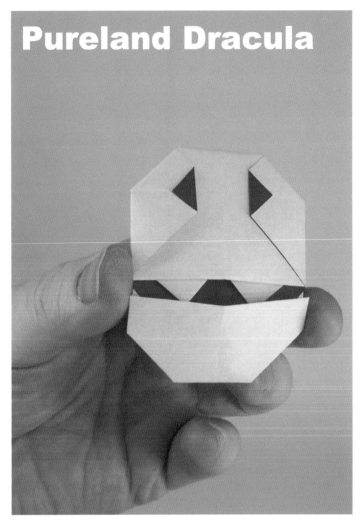

"Pureland" is where an origami model can be folded using only valley and mountain folds. It is surprising how effective some models can be when adhering to such simple rules.

Pureland Dracula

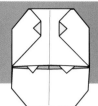

1

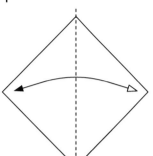

2

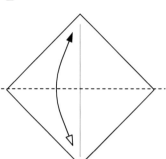

3

4

5

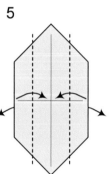

6

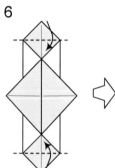

7

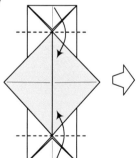

8

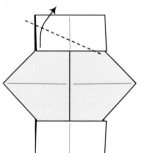

9

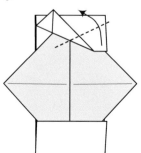

10

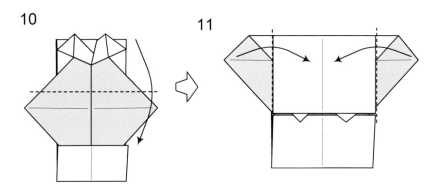

11

12

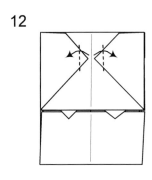

13

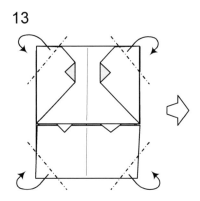

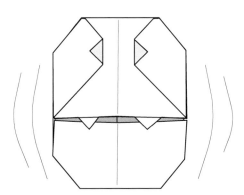

Press the sides and he bites!

The Grim Reaper

This model was designed in June 2002. It is dead easy to fold.

The Grim Reaper

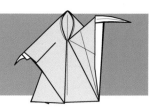

1

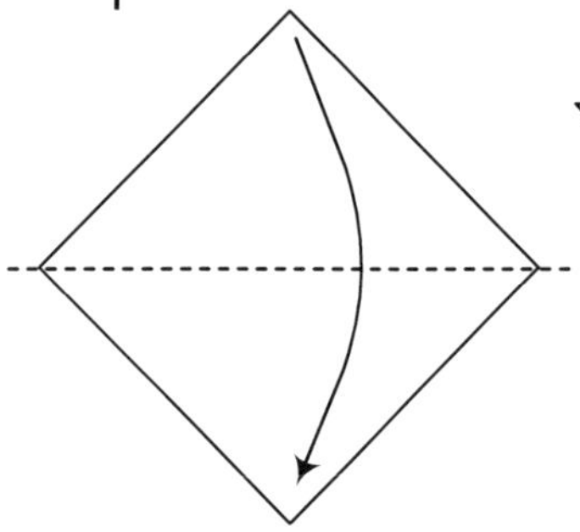

2

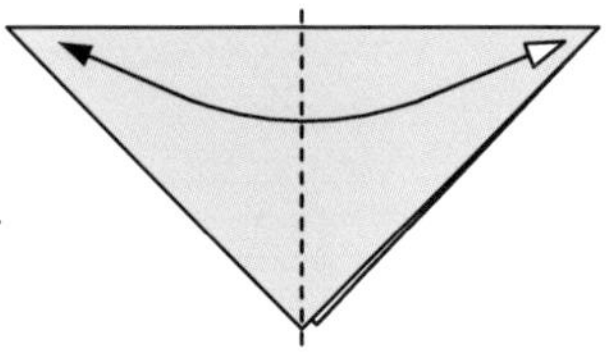

3

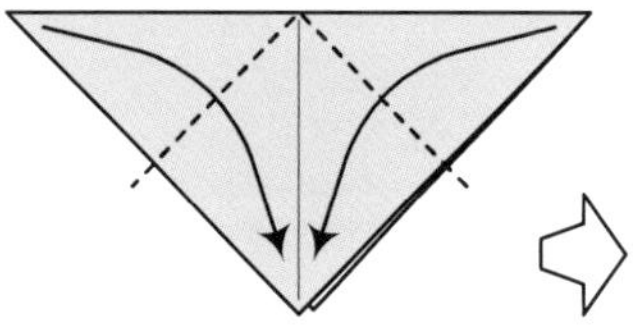

4

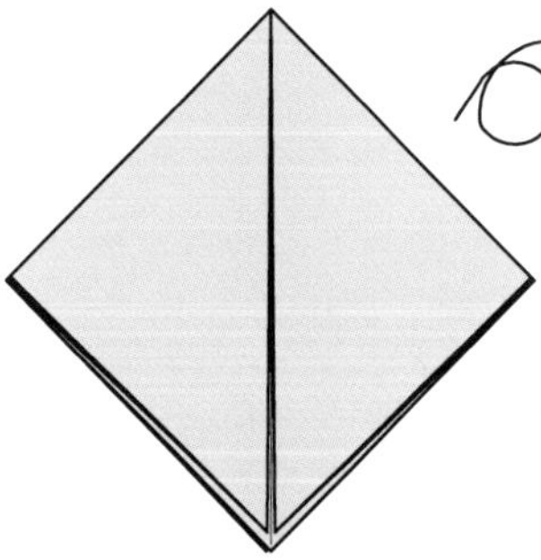

5

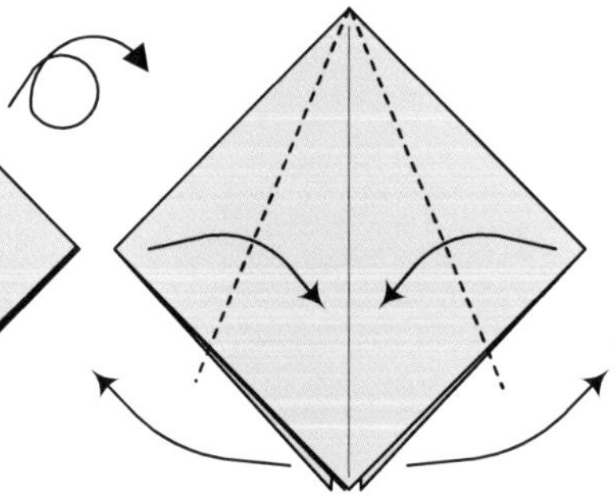

6

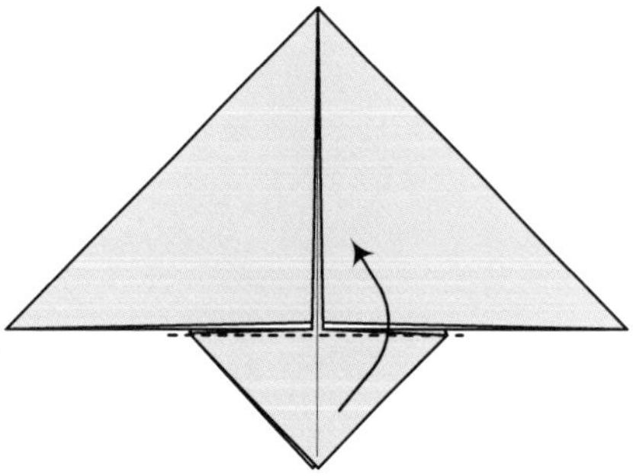

7

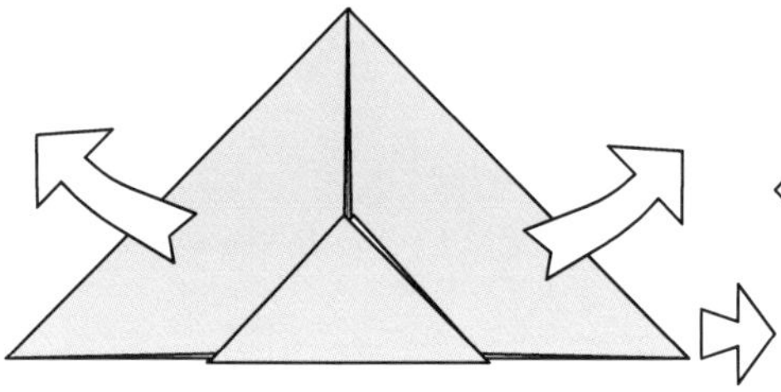

Unfold everything!

8

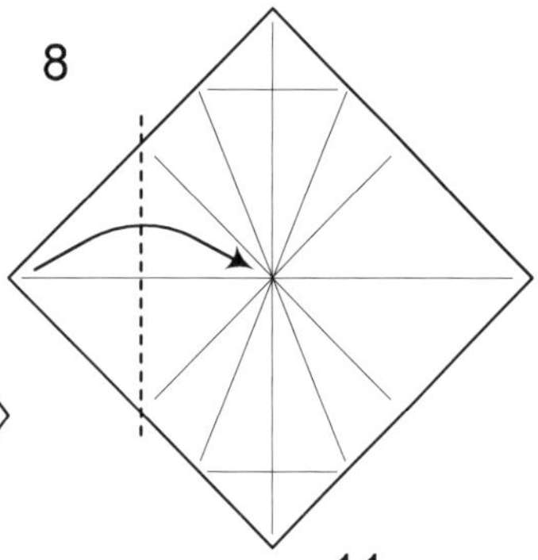

9

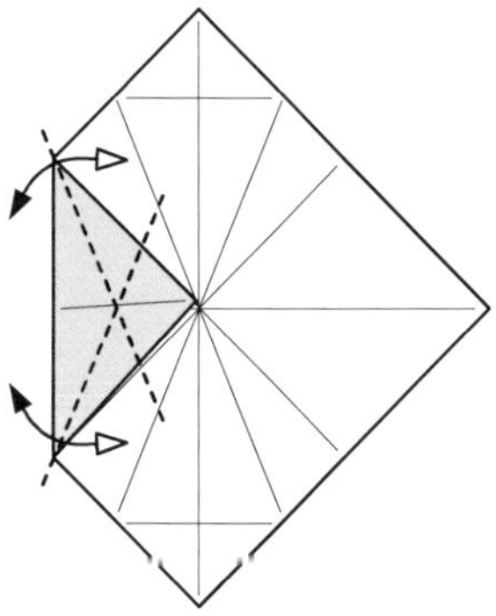

Crease single layer only

10

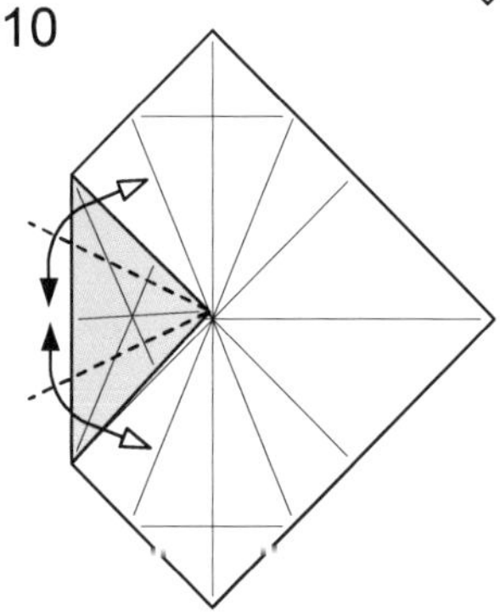

Crease single layer only

11

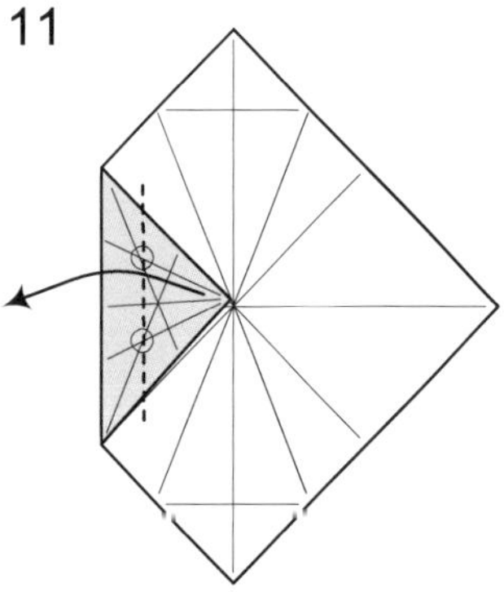

Fold using circled references

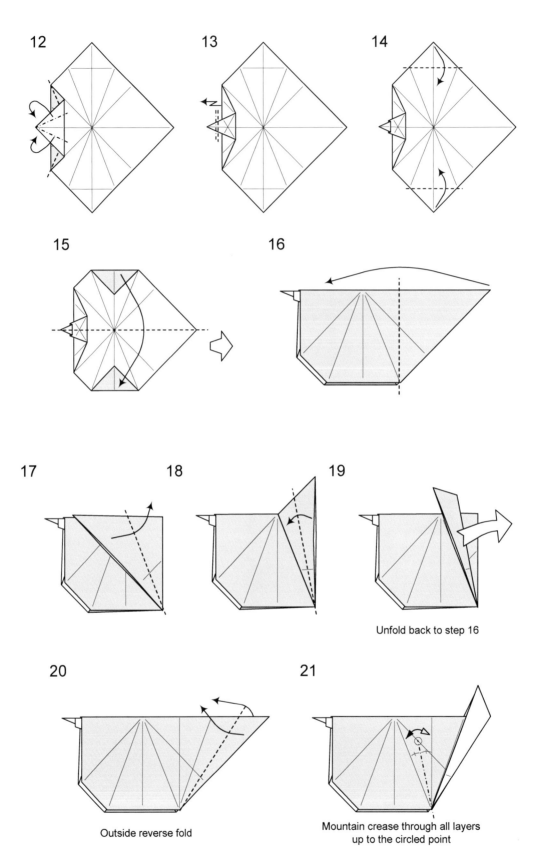

12

13

14

15

16

17

18

19

Unfold back to step 16

20

Outside reverse fold

21

Mountain crease through all layers
up to the circled point

22

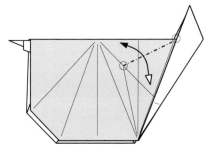

Another mountain crease

23

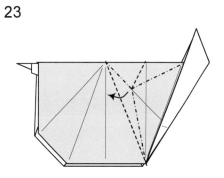

Rabbit ear on existing creases

24

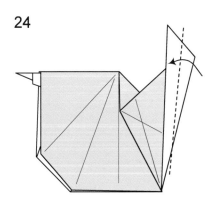

25

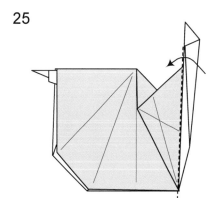

26

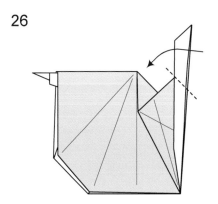

27

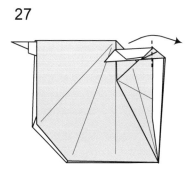

28

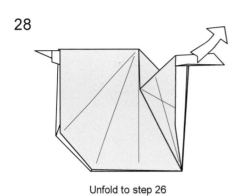

Unfold to step 26

29

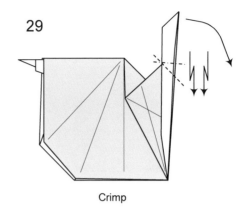

Crimp

30

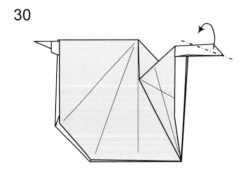

31

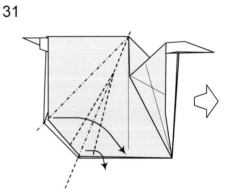

Fold arm using existing creases, but incorporate a small reverse fold on the top layer only. This will help the model to stand up.

32

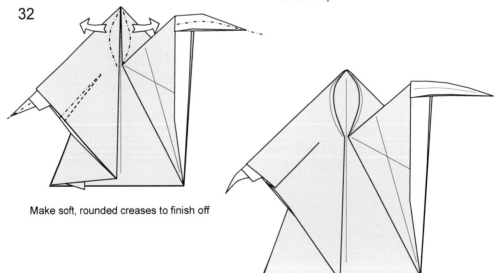

Make soft, rounded creases to finish off

Greed

I always enjoy action models. This one, designed in January 2003 was for a Valentine's challenge at an origami meeting in London. Rather than something romantic and heart shaped, I went for someone stuffing their face with chocolates. Sorry for any purists who object to sticking eyes on a model, it just works better this way.

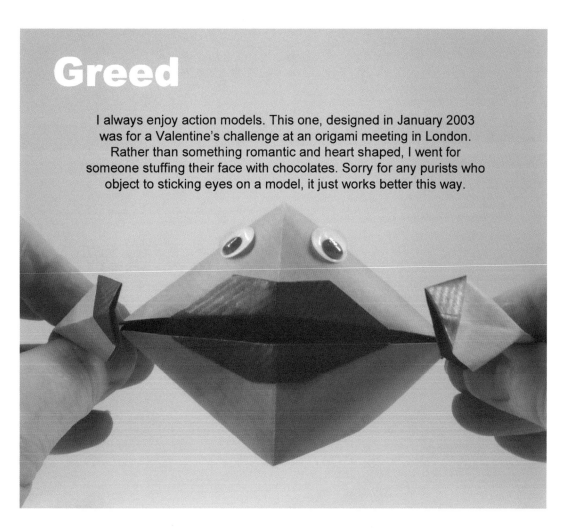

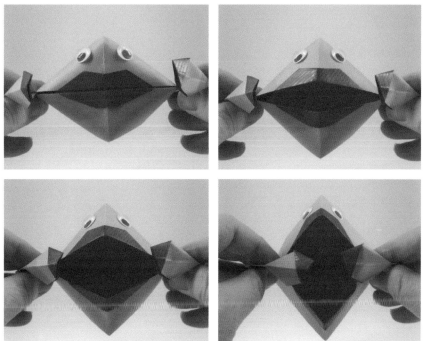

Greed

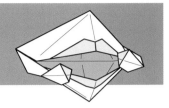

1

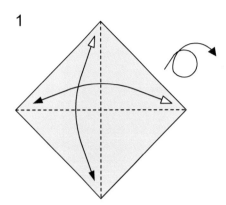

2

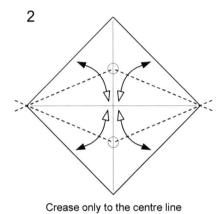

Crease only to the centre line

3

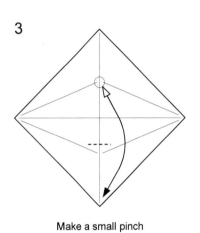

Make a small pinch

4

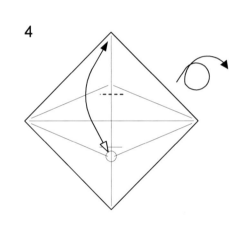

5

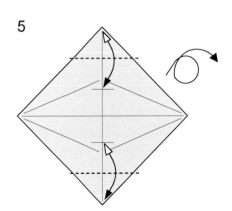

Crease up to the pinch marks

6

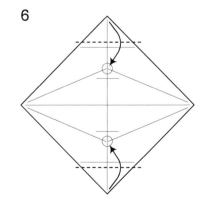

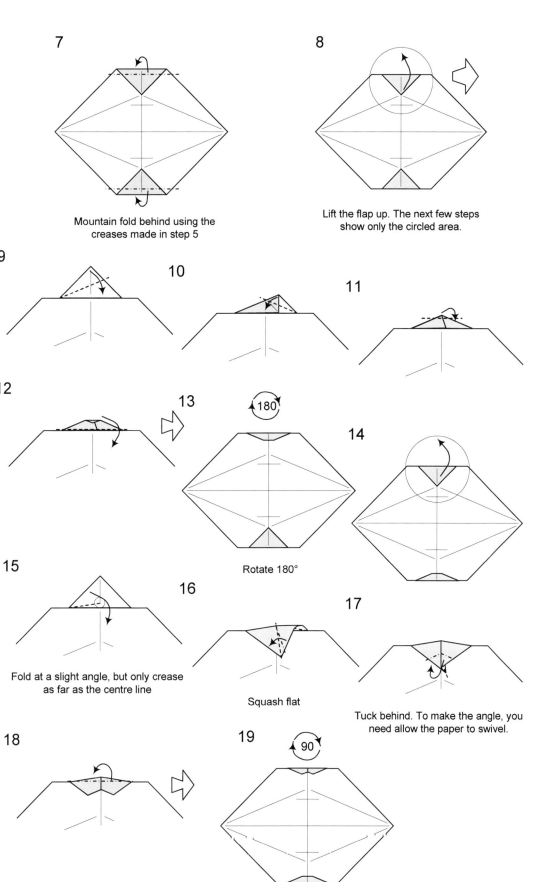

7

Mountain fold behind using the creases made in step 5

8

Lift the flap up. The next few steps show only the circled area.

9

10

11

12

13

180

Rotate 180°

14

15

Fold at a slight angle, but only crease as far as the centre line

16

Squash flat

17

Tuck behind. To make the angle, you need allow the paper to swivel.

18

19

90

20

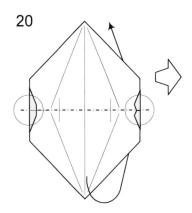

Mountain fold, but try not to crease too firmly in the circled areas

21

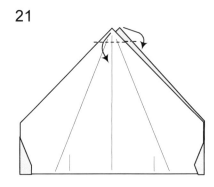

Fold the tips of the corners down a little

22

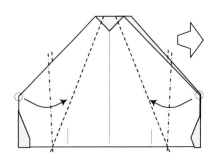

Crimp so the circled points lie on the diagonal lines

23

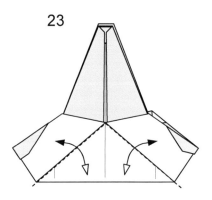

Crease through both layers, in both directions (mountain and valley)

24

Make 2 large rabbit ears, pulling the points apart and making the model 3-dimensional

25

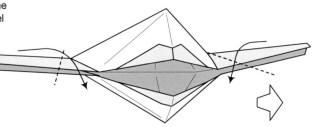

Valley folds

26

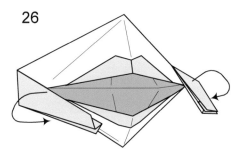

Wrap a single layer behind (the same as refolding step 25 as an outside reverse fold)

27

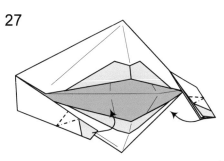

Squash folds to shape the hands, the creases do not have to be sharp

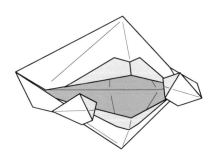

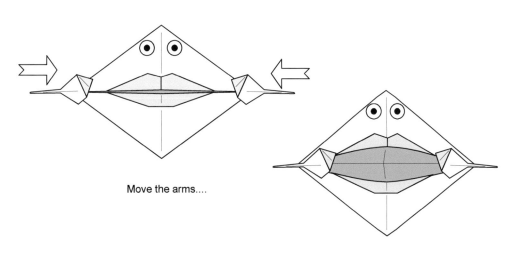

Move the arms....

...and her mouth opens

Teddy Bear

This Teddy Bear is the first model somebody asked me to design. I do not know the exact date this was created, but I think it was around 1993. He has evolved slightly over the years, and I have created a few variations. For instance, I can replace the jacket and tie, with a heart. He can also become a smartly dressed elephant!

Teddy Bear

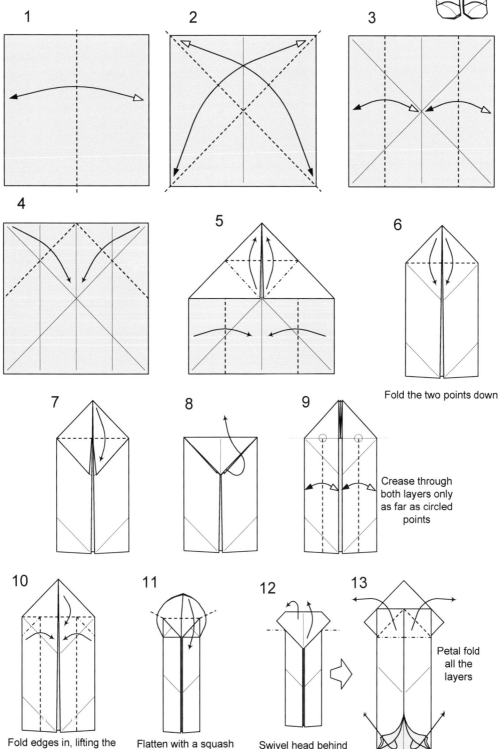

1

2

3

4

5

6

Fold the two points down

7

8

9

Crease through both layers only as far as circled points

10

Fold edges in, lifting the top point toward you

11

Flatten with a squash fold

12

Swivel head behind

13

Petal fold all the layers

14

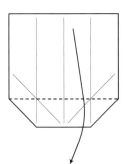

15

Swivel head to the front

16

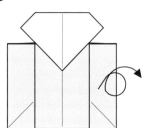

17

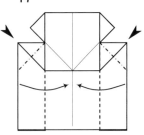

Squash fold while folding the
double layers to the centre line

18

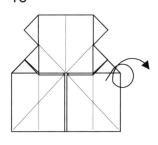

19

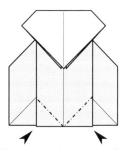

Make two inside reverse folds

20

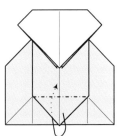

Tuck the point up inside the
model

21

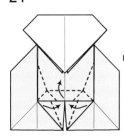

Petal fold

These 2 steps
are optional -
they are used to
extend the gap
between the legs

22

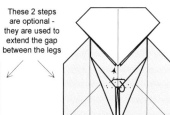

Reverse the point up inside the
model

23

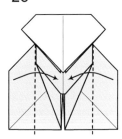

24

25

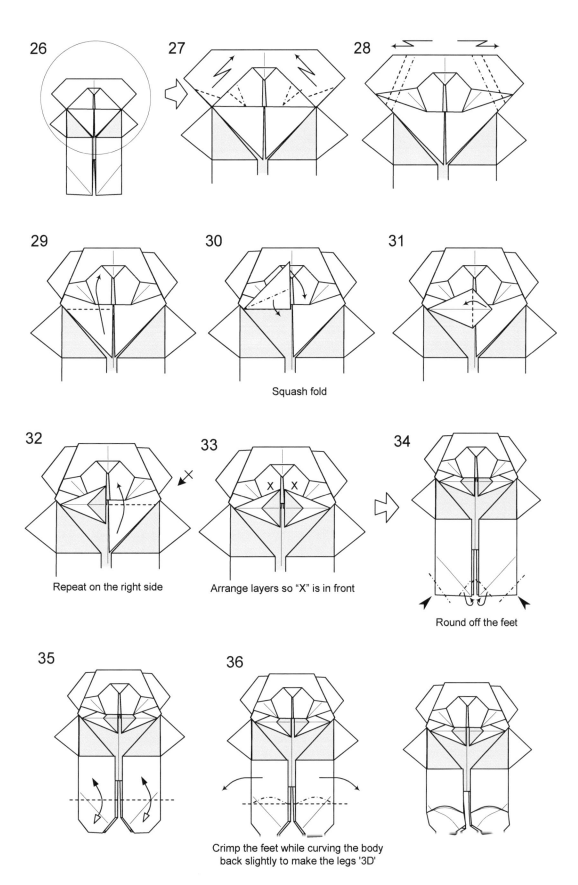

26

27

28

29

30

31

Squash fold

32

Repeat on the right side

33

Arrange layers so "X" is in front

34

Round off the feet

35

36

Crimp the feet while curving the body
back slightly to make the legs '3D'

Cat

This cat was designed in January 1999. Cat models in origami are quite rare, and I wanted to create one that looked like a witch's cat. The finishing and shaping of this model allow the folder to add some character. My one appears to be staring into nowhere with a blank expression, so quite autobiographical.

Cat

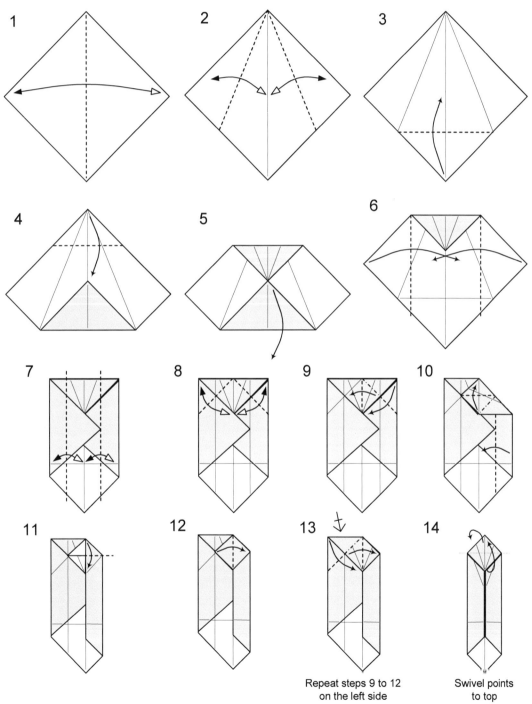

1

2

3

4

5

6

7

8

9

10

11

12

13

14

Repeat steps 9 to 12
on the left side

Swivel points
to top

15
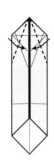

16

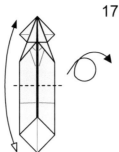

17
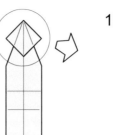
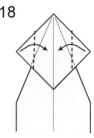

18

19
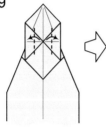

20
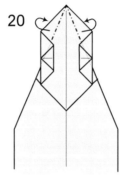

Fold 1 layer behind

21
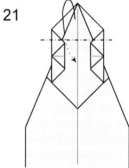

Fold point down
inside model

22
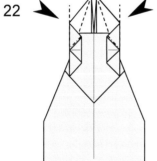

23
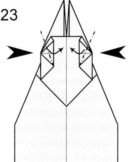

Squash folds

24
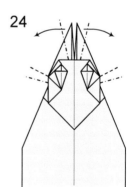

Swivel the ears
(keeping double layer at the front)

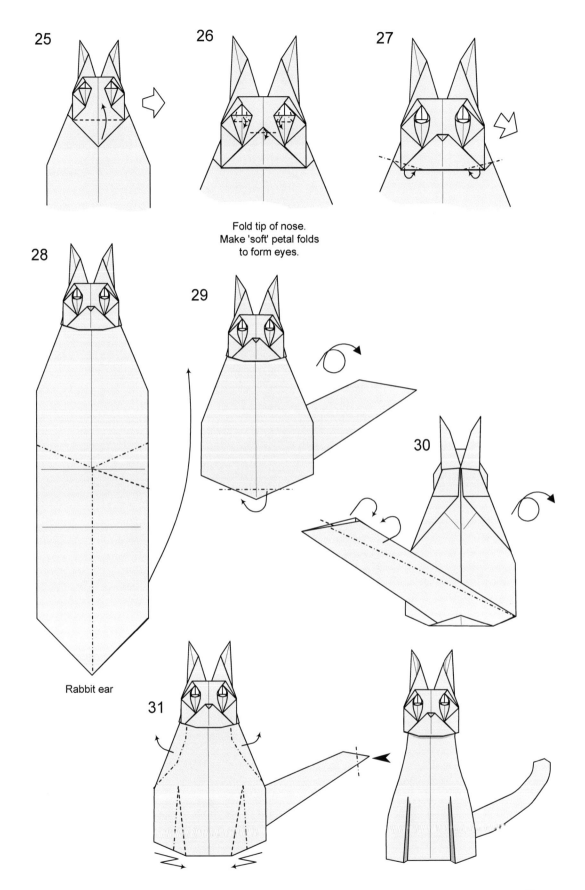

25

26

Fold tip of nose.
Make 'soft' petal folds
to form eyes.

27

28

29

30

31

Rabbit ear

The Frog Prince

This is a fun model to fold. The main steps are reasonably
straight forward, but the finishing touches are sculptural.
I designed the frog prince in February 2000. It was only as I
prepared this book, that I noticed that I have made so many
child-like models. Not sure what that says about me.

The Frog Prince

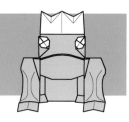

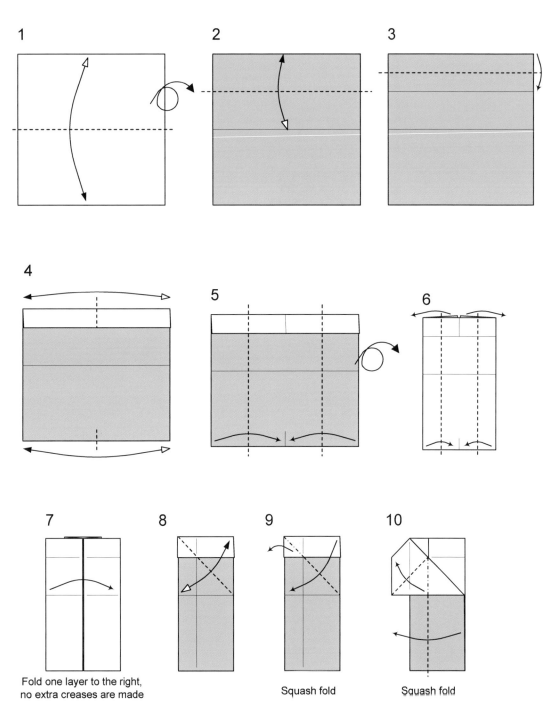

7 Fold one layer to the right, no extra creases are made

8

9 Squash fold

10 Squash fold

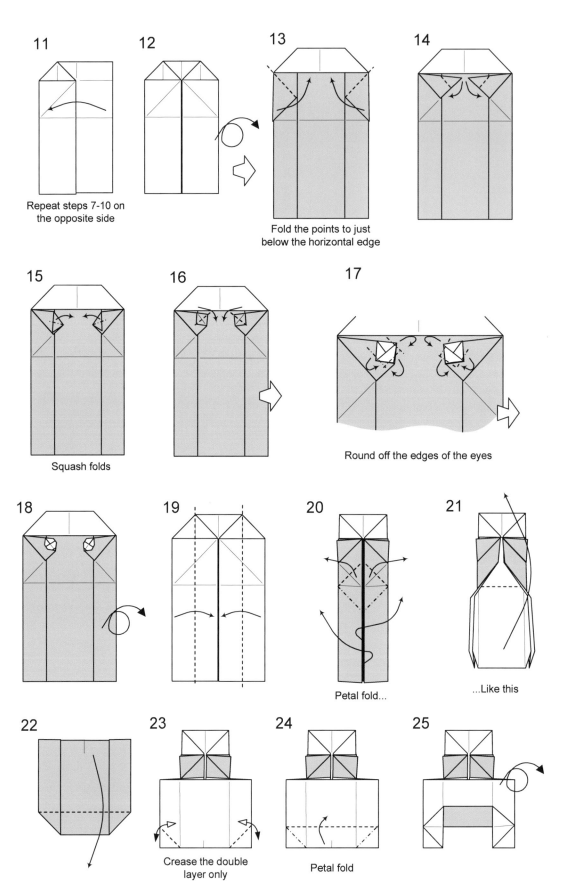

11 Repeat steps 7-10 on the opposite side

12

13 Fold the points to just below the horizontal edge

14

15 Squash folds

16

17 Round off the edges of the eyes

18

19

20 Petal fold...

21 ...Like this

22

23 Crease the double layer only

24 Petal fold

25

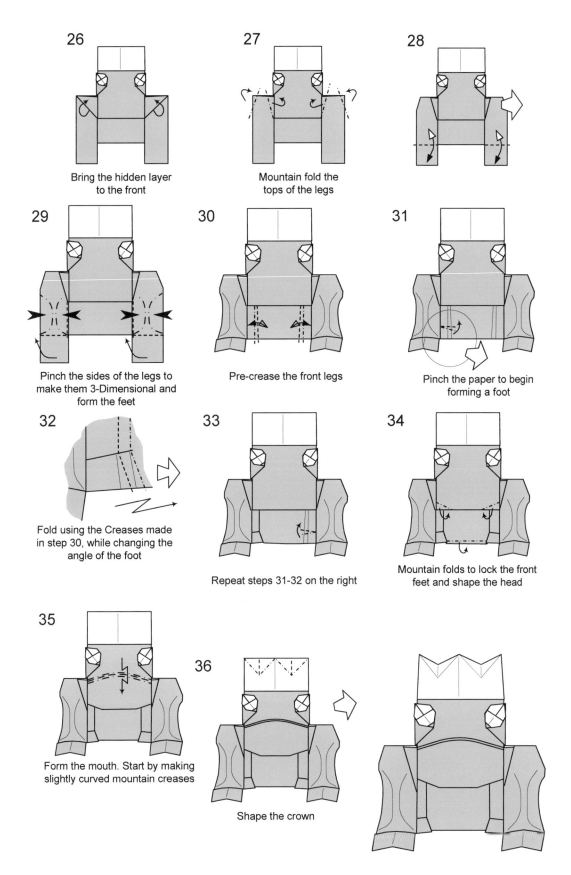

26 Bring the hidden layer to the front

27 Mountain fold the tops of the legs

28

29 Pinch the sides of the legs to make them 3-Dimensional and form the feet

30 Pre-crease the front legs

31 Pinch the paper to begin forming a foot

32 Fold using the Creases made in step 30, while changing the angle of the foot

33 Repeat steps 31-32 on the right

34 Mountain folds to lock the front feet and shape the head

35 Form the mouth. Start by making slightly curved mountain creases

36 Shape the crown

Monkey Head

This model was diagrammed in May 2004. It was designed in January for a meeting where the theme was the Chinese New Year (2004 was the year of the Monkey). It is quite easy to fold, but not quite so easy to fold neatly. Equally challenging is trying to find origami paper that is coloured appropriately on both sides.

Monkey Head

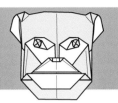

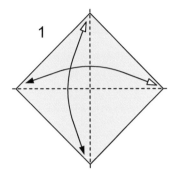

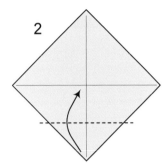

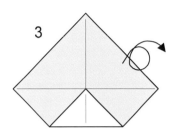

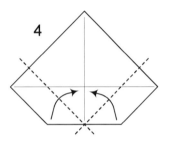

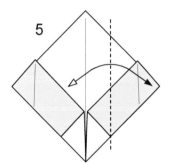

Reverse fold

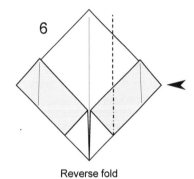

Reverse fold

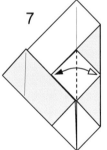

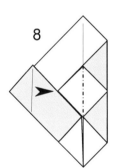

Reverse fold

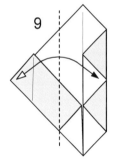

Repeat steps 5-8 on the other side

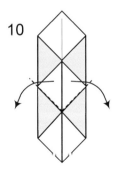

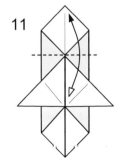

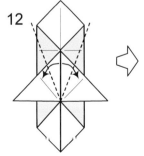

Fold the edges, the model will not lie flat

13

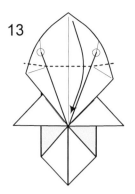

Fold the point down using step 11 as a guide. The model will no longer lie flat. The circled areas should be 'popped' inside out as the flap is folded down.

14

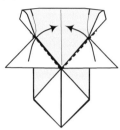

15

Make a small swivel fold

16

Swivel the other side to match

17

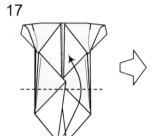

Valley fold, allowing the flap behind to flip to the front

18

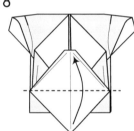

19

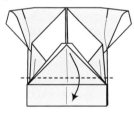

20

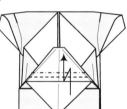

21

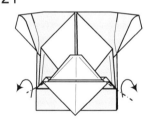

2 small mountain folds to lock the mouth

22

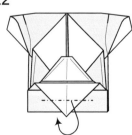

23

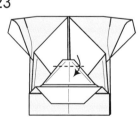

24

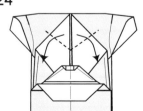

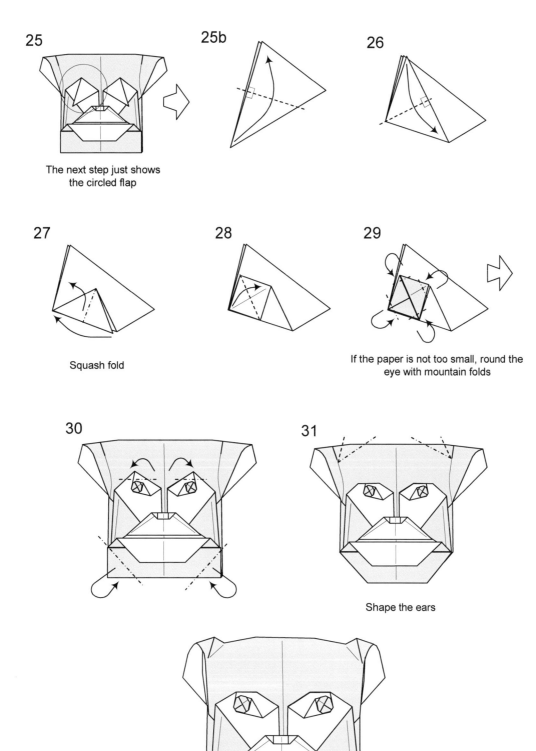

25

The next step just shows
the circled flap

25b

26

27

Squash fold

28

29

If the paper is not too small, round the
eye with mountain folds

30

31

Shape the ears

Fish

I designed this fish in a doctor's waiting room in November 2017.
I usually keep some 7.5cm origami paper in my wallet, so if I am ever
waiting, then I can occupy myself creatively. There is a lot of room
for modification with this design and if you are prepared to break
the purity of an origami model, a stick-on wiggly eye does wonders.

Fish

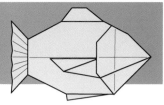

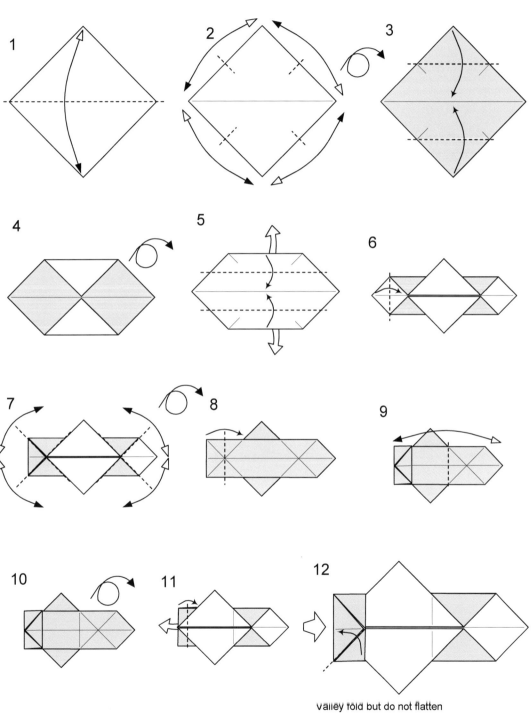

valley fold but do not flatten

13

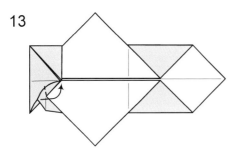

Valley fold but do not flatten

14

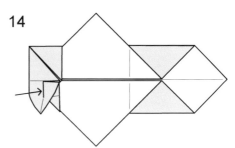

Firmly crease where indicated
then return to step 12

15

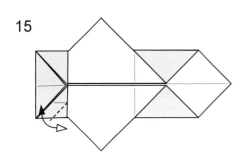

16

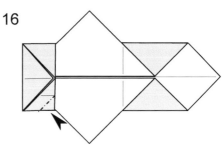

Inside reverse fold

17

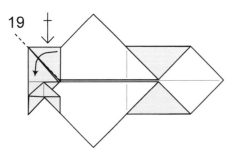

Valley fold, model will not quite flatten

18

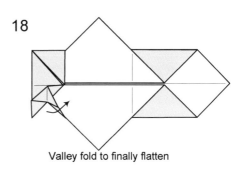

Valley fold to finally flatten

19

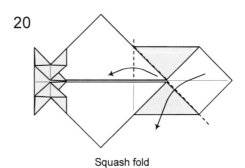

Repeat steps 12-18 on the other other
half of the tail

20

Squash fold

21

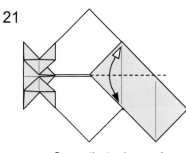

Crease the top layer only

22

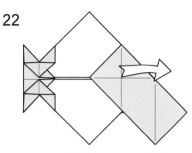

Unfold back to step 20

23

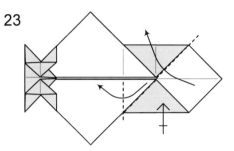

Repeat steps 20-22 on the other side

24

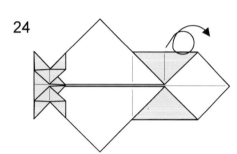

25

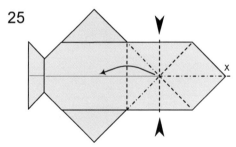

Collapse on existing creases, see step
26 for where point X moves to

26

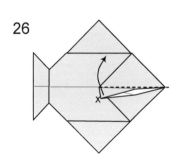

Valley fold the flap up to flatten

27

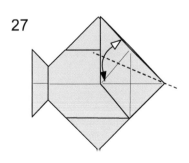

28

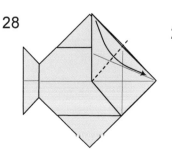

29

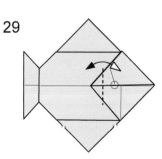

30

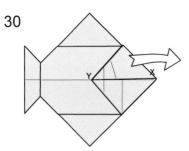

Open out the model slightly, point Y becomes the top of a pyramid

31

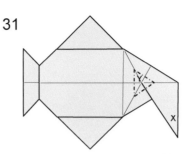

Push using creases made in step 29 to make an asymmetric sink

32

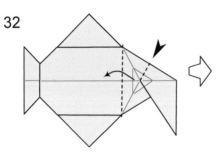

Keep the sink in place and return to step 29

33

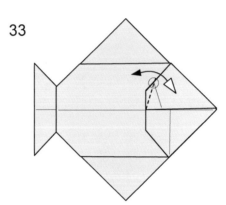

34

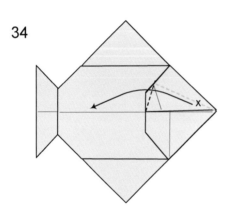

Petal fold point X as far to the left as possible

35

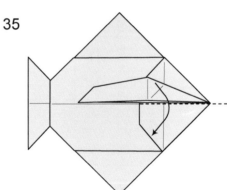

36

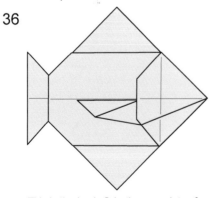

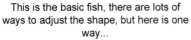

This is the basic fish, there are lots of ways to adjust the shape, but here is one way...

37

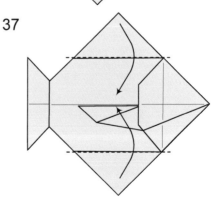

38

39

Rearrange the layers to hide the white
paper

40

41

42

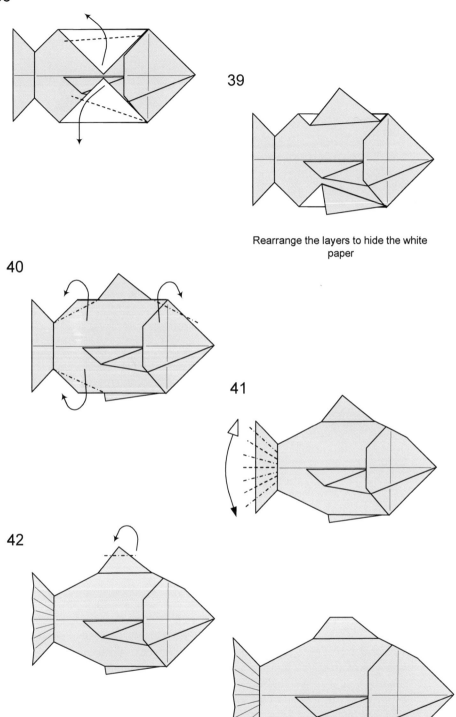

Badger

This badger was designed in September 1998. At that time, I was unaware of any other badger models, so I considered it a gap in the market. I usually avoid subjects that have been extensively explored by other origami designers. Having said that, it can also be a worthwhile challenge to come up with a novel twist on a familiar subject.

Badger

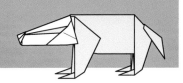

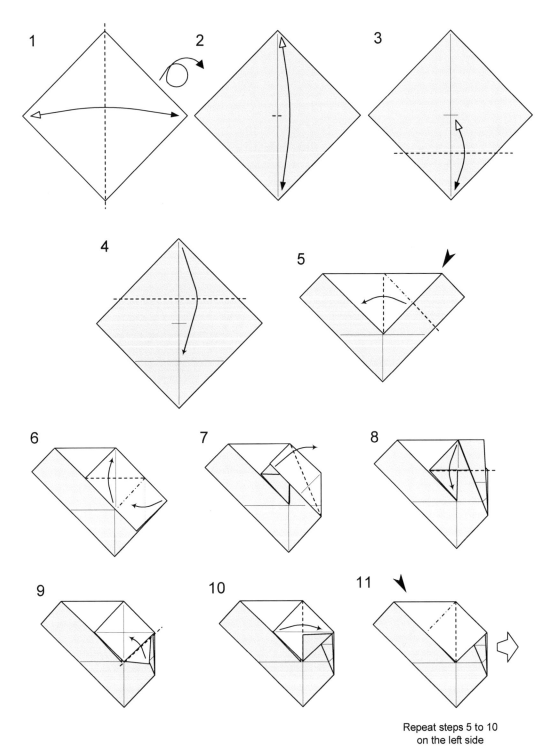

Repeat steps 5 to 10
on the left side

12

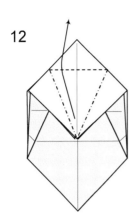

13

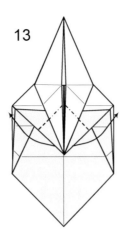

Inside reverse folds

14

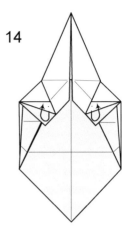

Wrap one layer to the front
(colour change)

15

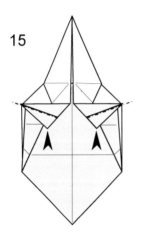

16

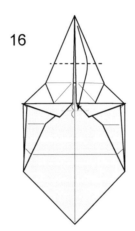

17

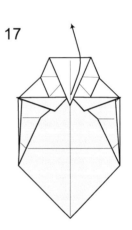

18

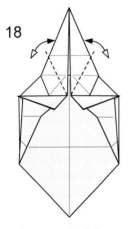

Crease a single layer

19

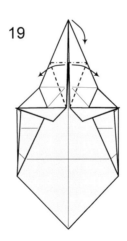

20

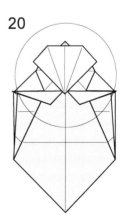

21

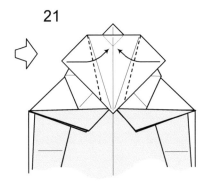

Fold sides towards the
base of the 'imaginary' square

22

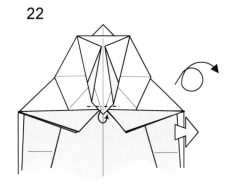

23

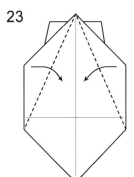

24

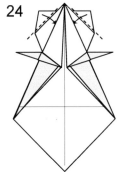

25

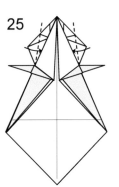

26

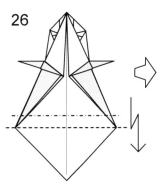

27

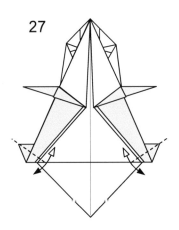

28

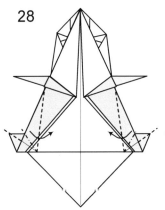

29

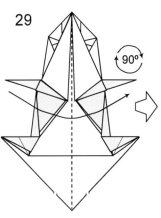

90°

30

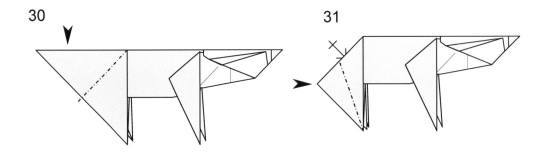

31

32

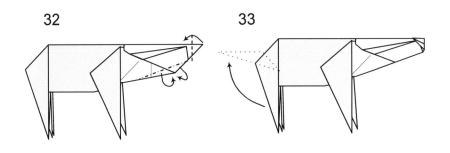

33

34

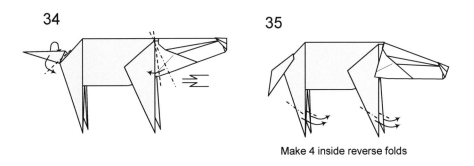

35

Make 4 inside reverse folds

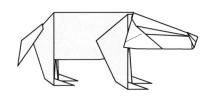

Spider

I designed this model in April 2001. In an idle moment, I drew a cartoon spider. Naturally, I considered an origami version which resulted in this fellow. Spiders having 8 legs, tend to be complex models. Pleating the legs has simplified things, but it is still not as easy as I would like. Perhaps in the future, if I can clear the cobwebs in my brain, I will see if I can put a new spin on things.

Spider

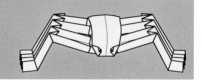

1

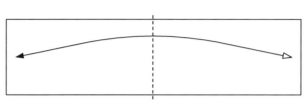

Begin with a 4x1 rectangle, crease in half

2

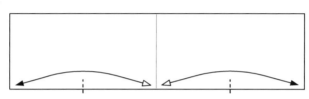

Lightly pinch 2 small creases

3

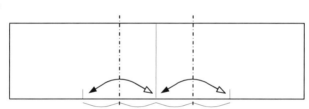

Make 2 mountain creases

4

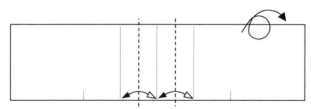

2 more valley creases, then turn over

5

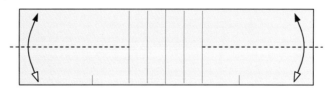

Try not to crease the middle section

6

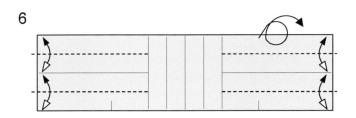

7

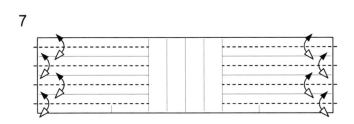

8

9

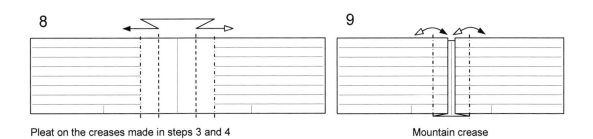

Pleat on the creases made in steps 3 and 4

Mountain crease

10

11

12

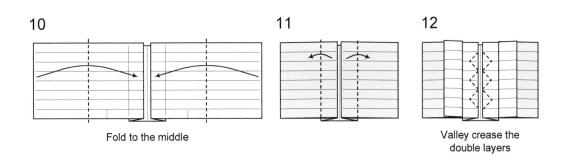

Fold to the middle

Valley crease the
double layers

13

14

15

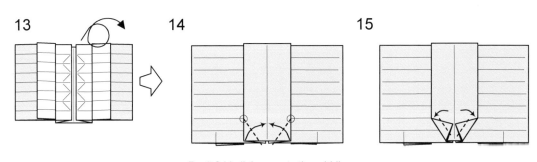

Don't fold all the way to the middle

16

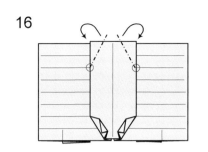

17

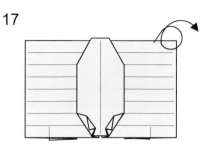

18

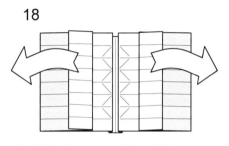

Unfold the 2 edges (not the middle)

19

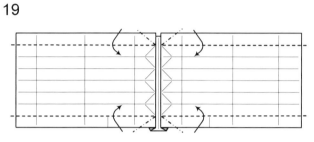

Squash folds

20

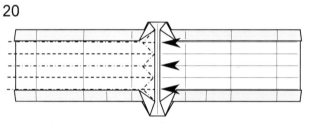

Pleat the legs (not the body). Sink diamond shapes as the model becomes 3 dimensional

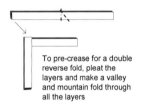

To pre-crease for a double reverse fold, pleat the layers and make a valley and mountain fold through all the layers

21

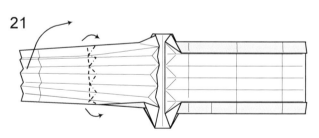

Double reverse fold to form a set of leg joints

22

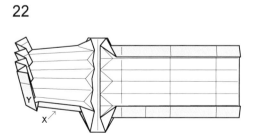

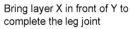

Bring layer X in front of Y to complete the leg joint

23

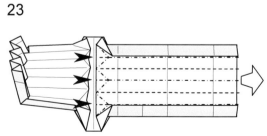

Repeat steps 20 - 22 on the right side

23

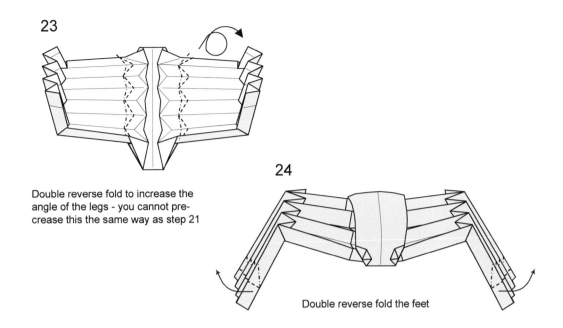

Double reverse fold to increase the
angle of the legs - you cannot pre-
crease this the same way as step 21

24

Double reverse fold the feet

25

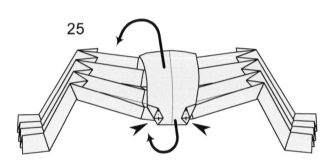

Make soft squash folds for the eyes
and curve the body

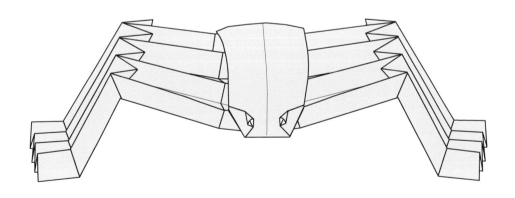

Monkey

I don't design a lot of origami animals, but I am quite pleased with this chap. He was created in March 2000. He can be folded with standard 15cm origami paper, but this example is from brown wrapping paper. His legs are a bit weak, so he won't stand up very easily.

Monkey

1

2

3

4

5

Crease the top layer only

6

Unfold

7

Form a waterbomb base

8

Bisect the angle

9

Pleat again

10

Unfold to step 8

11

Make 4 inside reverse folds
on existing creases

12

Repeat steps 8-11 on the left side

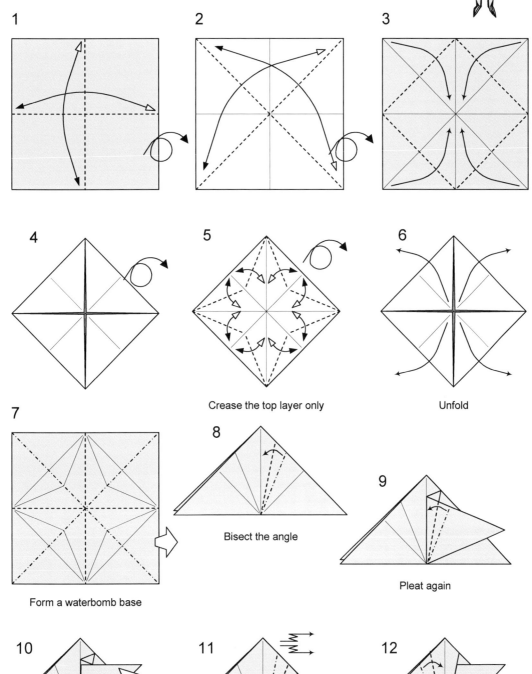

115

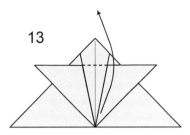

13

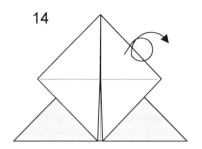

14

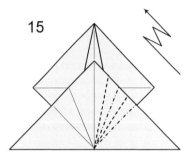

15

Double pleat (like steps 8-9)

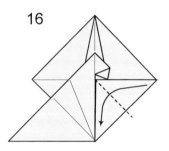

16

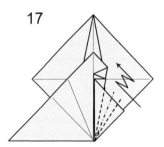

17

Double pleat the 4 layers

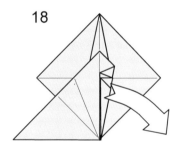

18

Unfold to step 15

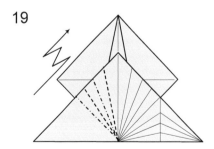

19

Repeat steps 15 to 18 on the left side

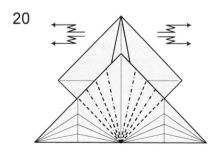

20

Make 2 sets of inside reverse folds, as in step 11

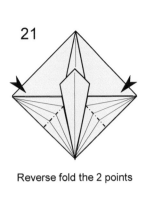

21

Reverse fold the 2 points

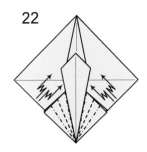

22

Finally, 4 more sets of
reverse folds

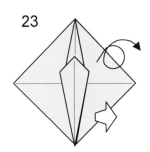

23

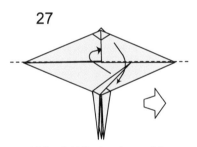

24

Fold the flap on the right first

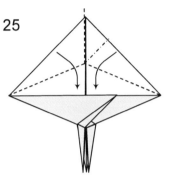

25

Rabbit ear

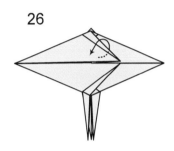

26

Wrap 1 layer over the point

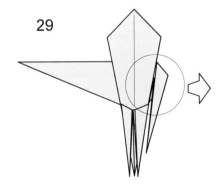

27

Valley fold the top down while
tucking the point behind to lock

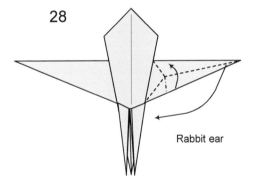

28

Rabbit ear

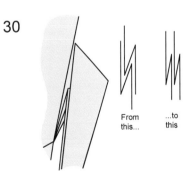

29

30

From
this...

...to
this

Separate the 2 inner layers, no
new creases are required

31

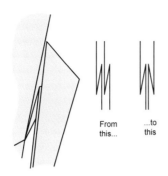

From this... ...to this

Reverse the existing creases
so the flap is inside the model

32

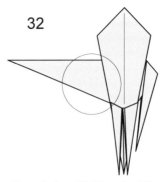

Repeat steps 28-31 on the left
side

33

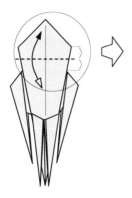

Make a sharp crease

34

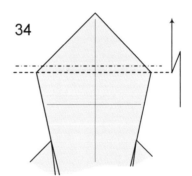

35

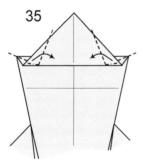

Narrow the sides

36

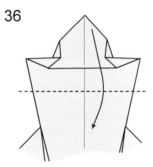

Fold the head down

37

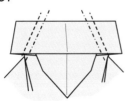

Valley and mountain fold each side
to make the ears

38

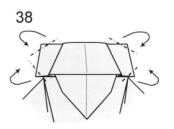

Round off the ears

39

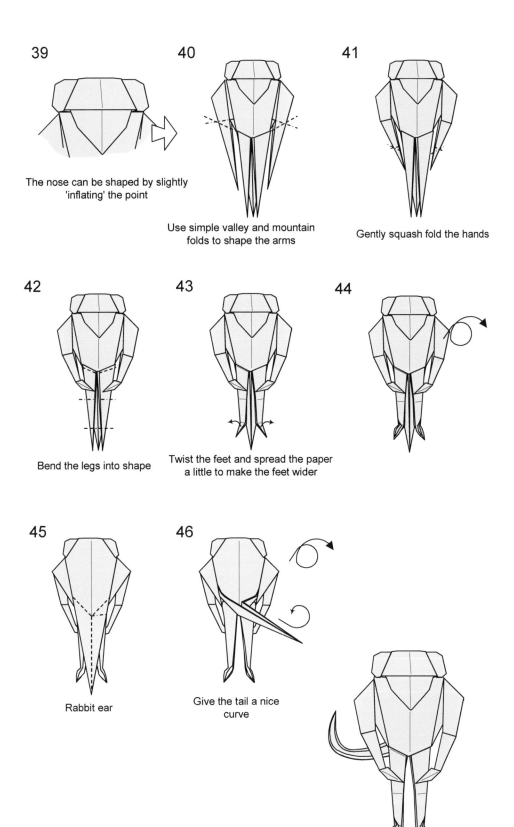

The nose can be shaped by slightly 'inflating' the point

40

Use simple valley and mountain folds to shape the arms

41

Gently squash fold the hands

42

Bend the legs into shape

43

Twist the feet and spread the paper a little to make the feet wider

44

45

Rabbit ear

46

Give the tail a nice curve

Dracula

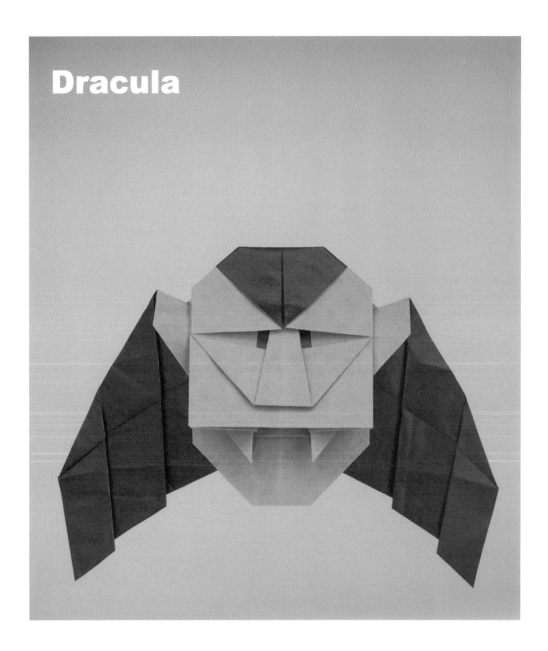

Designed in September 2001, this Dracula model is a good contrast
to the simplicity of the pureland model. He is fairly complex,
but can be folded from standard 15cm origami paper and the
end result is satisfying.

I wonder if it is possible to make a "scary" origami model? This chap
certainly isn't.

Dracula

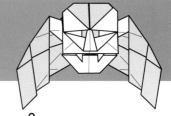

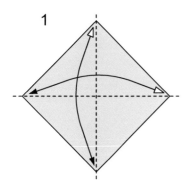

1

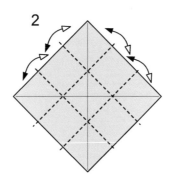

2

Crease into thirds

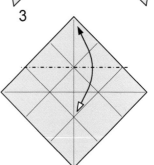

3

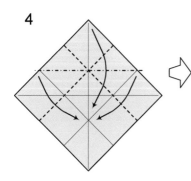

4

Preliminary fold

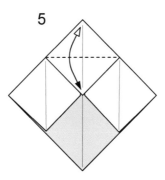

5

Crease the top layer

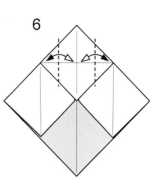

6

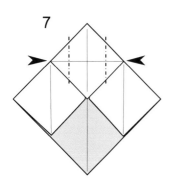

7

Inside reverse folds

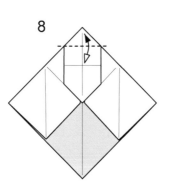

8

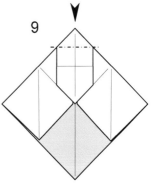

9

Sink

121

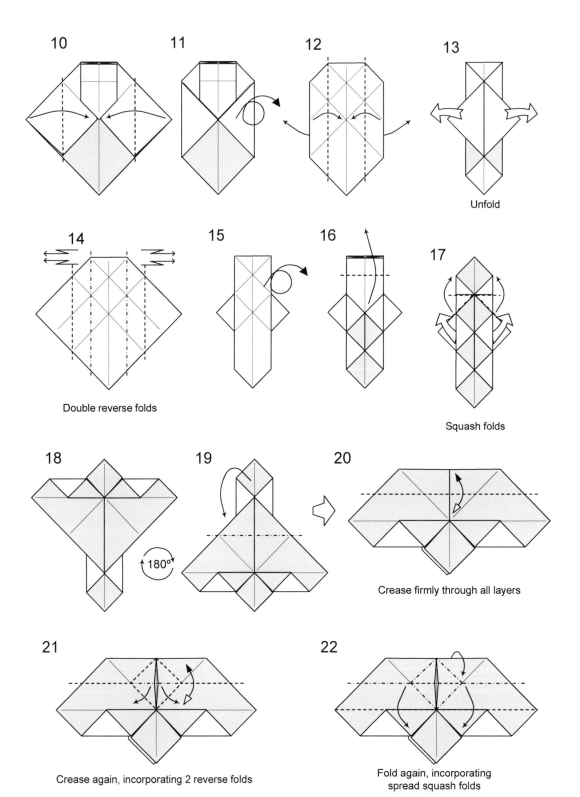

10

11

12

13

Unfold

14

Double reverse folds

15

16

17

Squash folds

18

180°

19

20

Crease firmly through all layers

21

Crease again, incorporating 2 reverse folds

22

Fold again, incorporating
spread squash folds

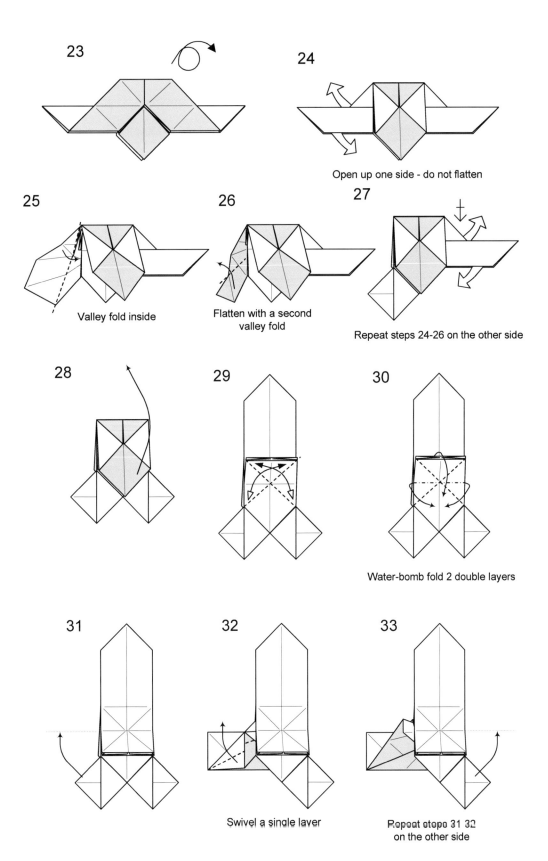

23

24

Open up one side - do not flatten

25

Valley fold inside

26

Flatten with a second
valley fold

27

Repeat steps 24-26 on the other side

28

29

30

Water-bomb fold 2 double layers

31

32

Swivel a single layer

33

Repeat steps 31-32
on the other side

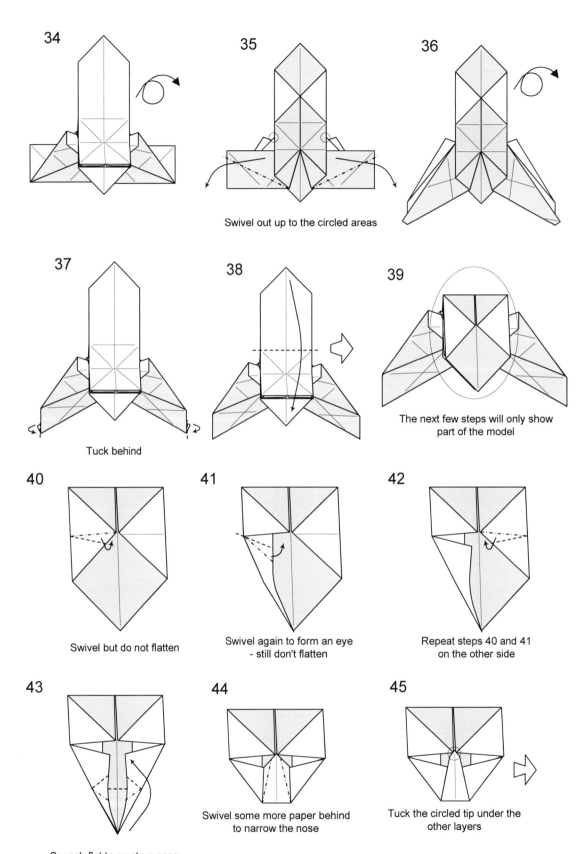

34

35

Swivel out up to the circled areas

36

37

Tuck behind

38

39

The next few steps will only show part of the model

40

Swivel but do not flatten

41

Swivel again to form an eye - still don't flatten

42

Repeat steps 40 and 41 on the other side

43

Squash flat to create a nose

44

Swivel some more paper behind to narrow the nose

45

Tuck the circled tip under the other layers

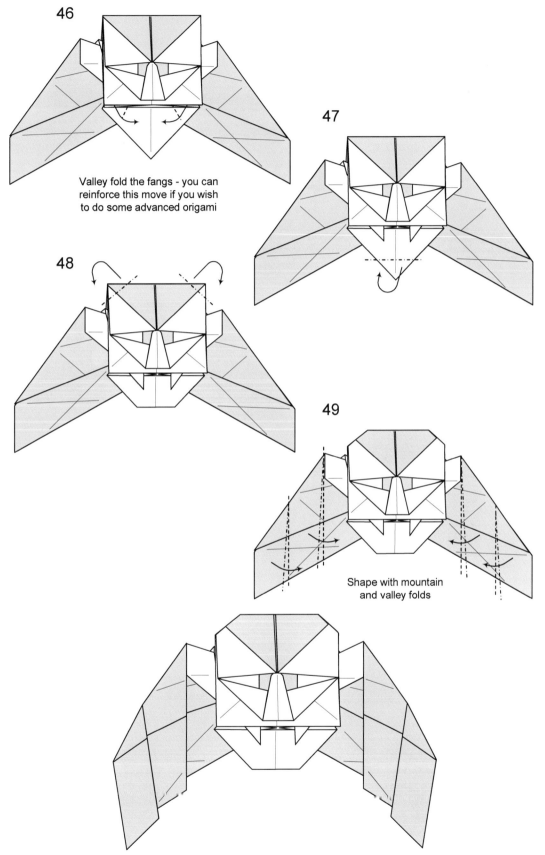

46

Valley fold the fangs - you can
reinforce this move if you wish
to do some advanced origami

47

48

49

Shape with mountain
and valley folds

Glynn's Glider

Glynn's Glider was designed in September 1997 in the bar at an origami convention in York. It was the night before a paper plane competition at a nearby aircraft hanger as part of the celebrations for the 30th anniversary of the British Origami Society. I wanted to get a streamlined plane with a bit of extra weight at the front. This plane held the British record for long distance (it went 96 feet) for about 10 minutes! The winner used some tape in his model, so this remains the unofficial record for pure origami.

Glynn's Glider

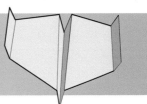

1

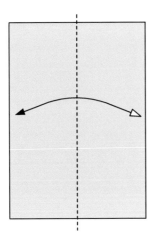

Start with a sheet of A sized paper

2

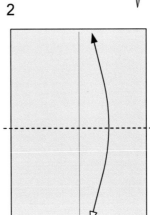

3

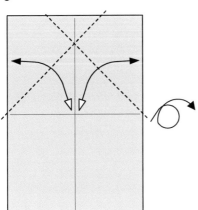

4

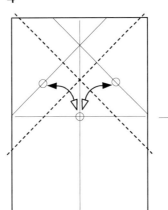

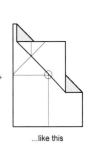

...like this

To line up the existing crease to the middle of the paper, re-fold a corner from step 1....

5

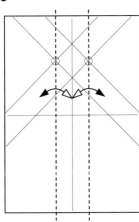

6

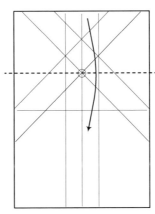

7

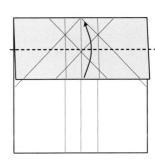

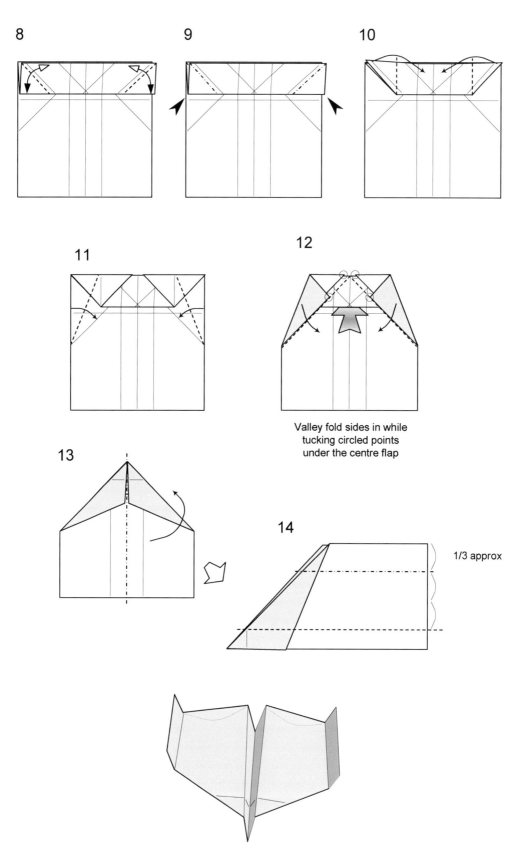

8   **9**   **10**

11   **12**

Valley fold sides in while
tucking circled points
under the centre flap

13

14

1/3 approx

If required, lightly raise the rear edges of
the wings

Fidget Spinner

Being quite a fan of gadgets, and something of a fidget myself, I bought a fidget spinner long before they became so popular. It did not seem a natural candidate for an origami model, but I thought it would be interesting to make a deliberately bad spinner. The result was this square version. Strangely though, it actually spins quite well.

Fidget Spinner

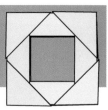

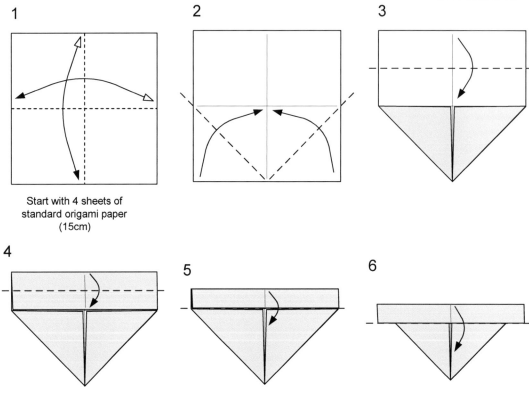

1

Start with 4 sheets of
standard origami paper
(15cm)

2

3

4

5

6

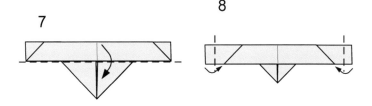

7

8

9

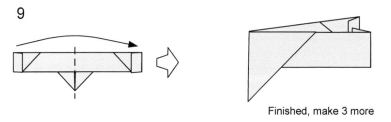

Finished, make 3 more

Assembly

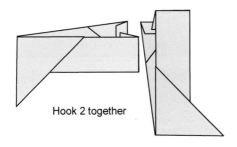

Hook 2 together

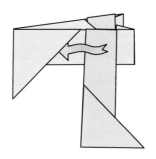

Slide (it helps to
keep things loose)

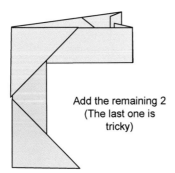

Add the remaining 2
(The last one is
tricky)

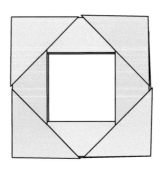

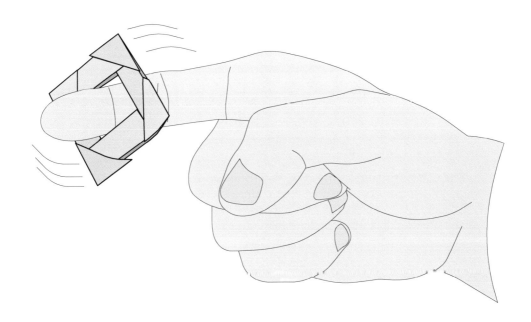

Big nose glider

This was designed in April 2005. It flies really well and has a solid and sturdy nose. As with any paper plane, the secret of a good glider is to fold with precision and then to make small adjustments to the shape until it glides well. A good start is to bend the back of the wings up slightly. Too much though, and it will fly with a dipping motion.

Big nose glider

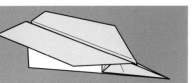

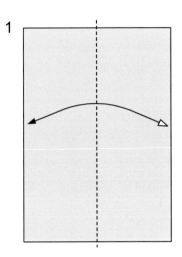

1

Start with a sheet of A4 (or any 1:1.414 rectangle), crease across the centre

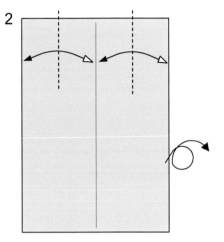

2

Divide into quarters, but do not crease the whole length of the paper

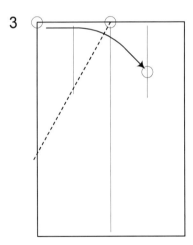

3

Valley fold the corner so that it touches the crease made in step 2

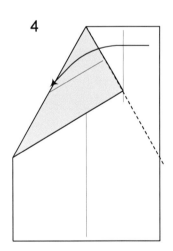

4

Fold the opposite edge over

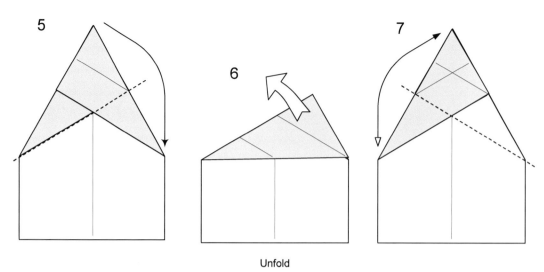

5

6

Unfold

7

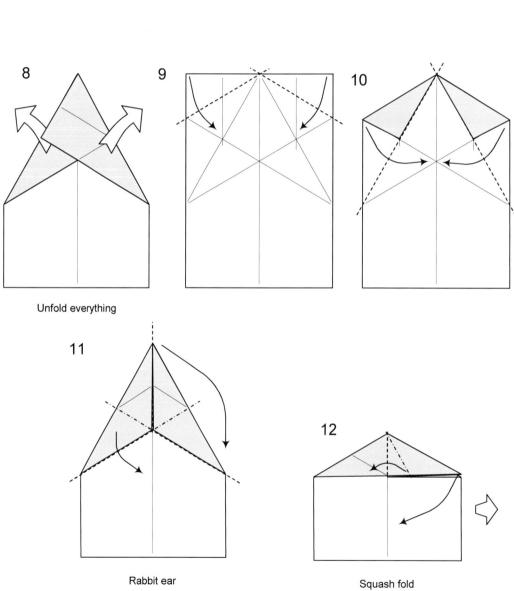

8

Unfold everything

9

10

11

Rabbit ear

12

Squash fold

13

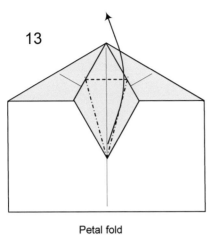

Petal fold

14   90°

Mountain fold the whole model

15

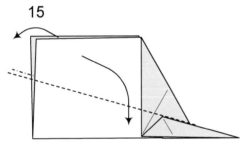

Fold the wings down using the nose as
a guide. (I usually make this angle very
slightly more shallow than the nose)

Profile

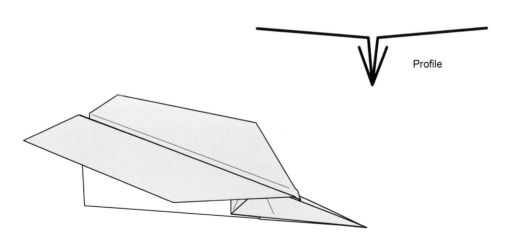

Throw firmly at a slightly downward angle

Office in tray

This is a very simple and practical model designed in June 2017.
This one was folded using large thin card and is very strong.

Office in tray

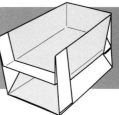

1

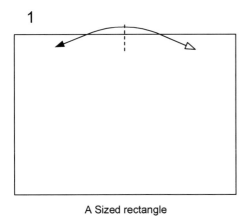

A Sized rectangle

2

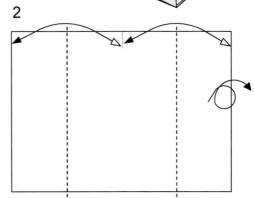

3

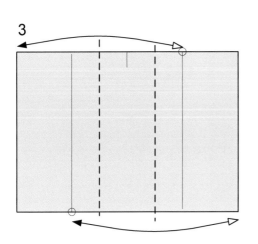

4

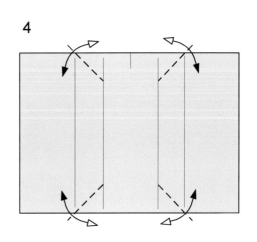

5

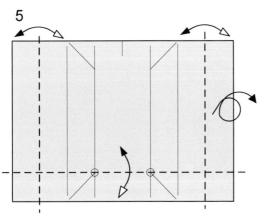

6

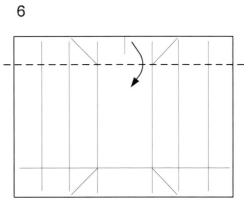

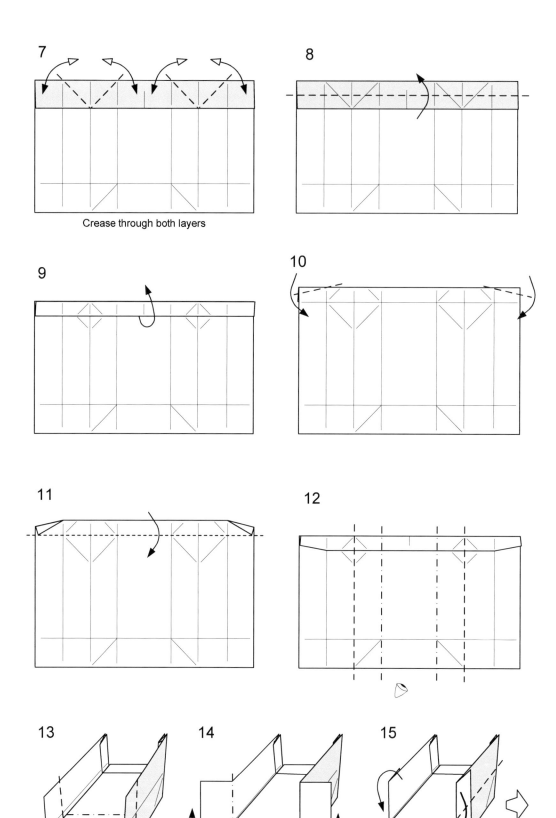

7

Crease through both layers

8

9

10

11

12

13

14

15

16

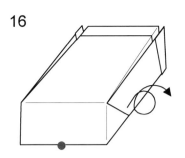

Turn over - follow the red spot
for the correct orientation

17

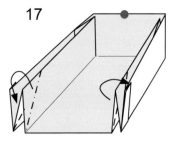

Mountain fold to lock sides

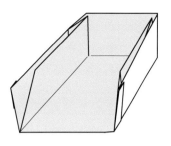

Lower tray complete

Upper Tray

1

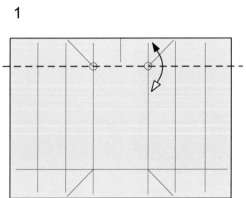

For the upper tray, begin by
folding up to step 5 of the
lower tray

2

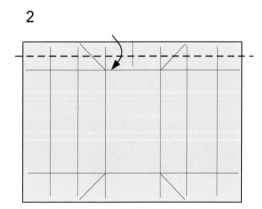

3

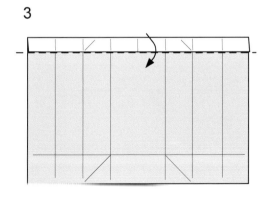

4

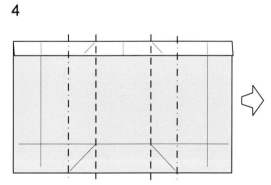

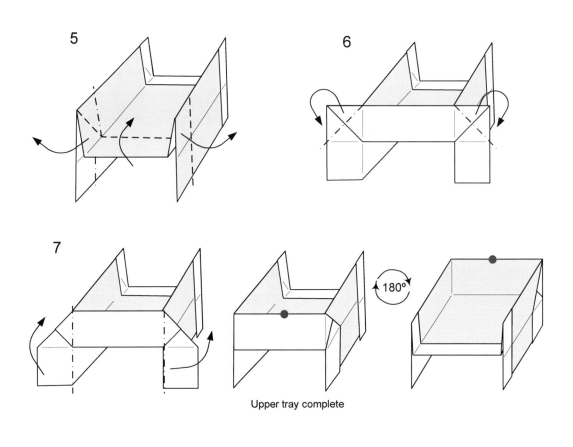

5

6

7

Upper tray complete

180°

Assembly

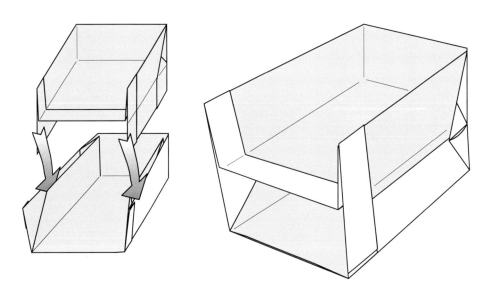

Flipper

Many years ago (in 1998), there was a free gift in a crisp packet which was constructed from card and flipped to show various pictures and pattern. They were quite popular for a short while.

Of course, I had to design an origami version. At the time I was happy with my design and so I diagrammed the model and that was that.

When I came to write this book, I revisited the design and thought that it had not aged very well. Rather than forget about it, I tried to come up with a better version.

This is the result. I really like the locking mechanism, the folding and assembly is fun, and it's great to play with if you are a bit of a fidget - which I am.

Flipper

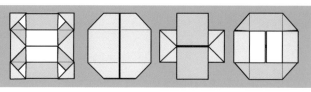

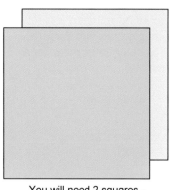

You will need 2 squares - different colours and/or patterns work well

1

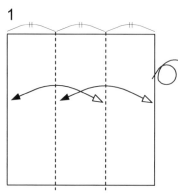

Divide into thirds

2

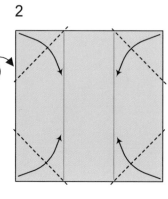

3

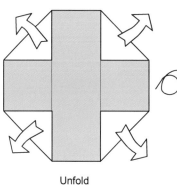

Unfold

4

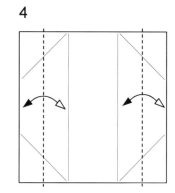

5

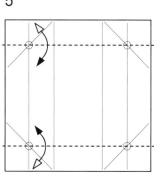

6

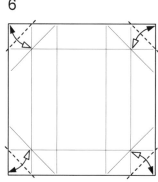

7

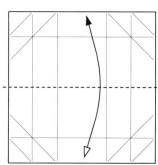

8

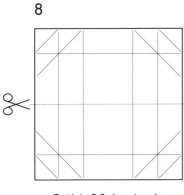

Cut into 2 2x1 rectangles

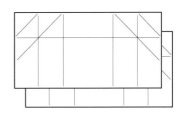

Use another square to
make 2 more

Folding and assembly

1

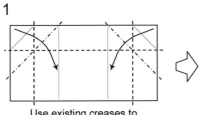

Use existing creases to
make 2 "preliminary" folds

2

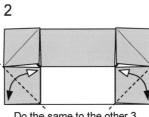

Do the same to the other 3
units

3

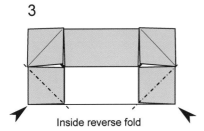

Inside reverse fold

4

Fold the other units the
same way

5

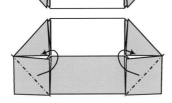

On 2 units, tuck the corners
under

6

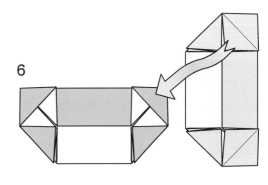

Place one of the remaining units
behind, just a single layer goes in
front

7

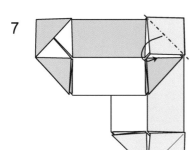

Use the existing mountain
fold to lock

8

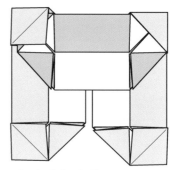

Lock all 4 units the same way

9

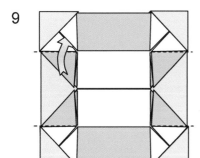

Tuck each of the triangular flaps
into a pocket

10

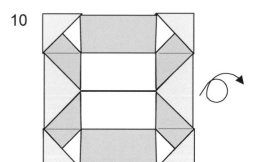

11

Tuck in the remaining 4
triangular flaps

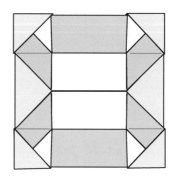

Complete

How it works - the 4 positions

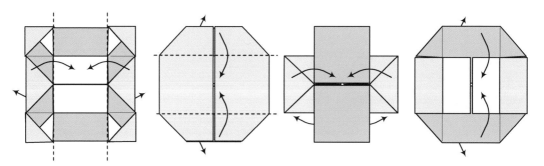

Tower Bridge

I designed this model of Tower Bridge in 2006, when I was invited
to attend an origami convention in the Netherlands. I wanted to
contribute a model that reflected where I come from. I could not
think of anything from my home town of Harlow, but I am close
enough to London to justify this model.

Tower Bridge

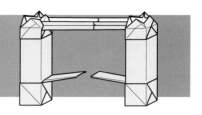

1

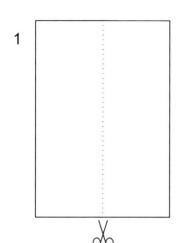

Begin with 2 halves of a sheet of A4. It's best if the paper is the same colour on both sides

2

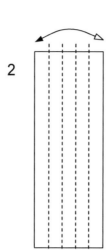

Valley fold into fifths

3

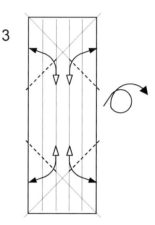

Valley creases -only crease the first 2 segments on each side

4

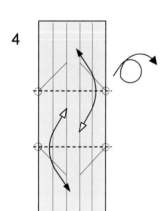

5

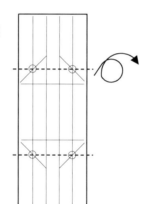

6

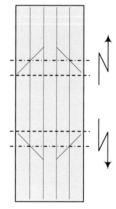

7

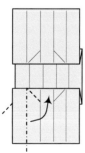

Do not flatten completely

8

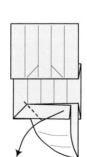

9

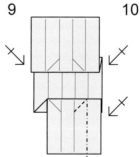

Repeat steps 7-8 on the other 3 edges

10

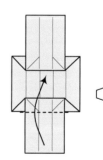

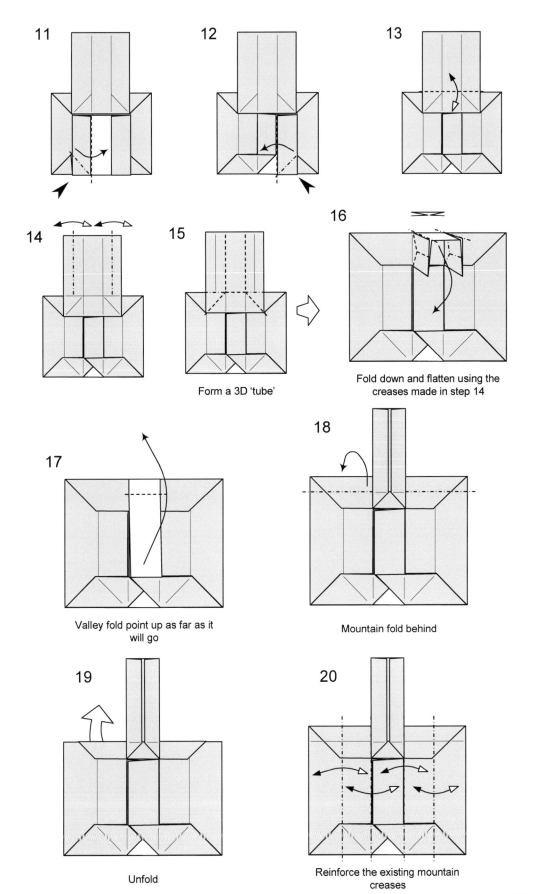

11

12

13

14

15

Form a 3D 'tube'

16

Fold down and flatten using the
creases made in step 14

17

Valley fold point up as far as it
will go

18

Mountain fold behind

19

Unfold

20

Reinforce the existing mountain
creases

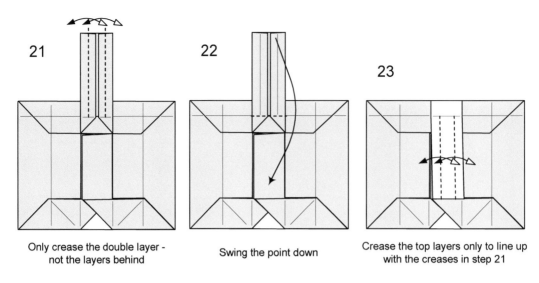

21

Only crease the double layer -
not the layers behind

22

Swing the point down

23

Crease the top layers only to line up
with the creases in step 21

24

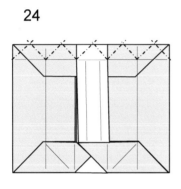

Make small mountain creases

25

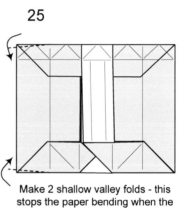

Make 2 shallow valley folds - this
stops the paper bending when the
model is assembled

26

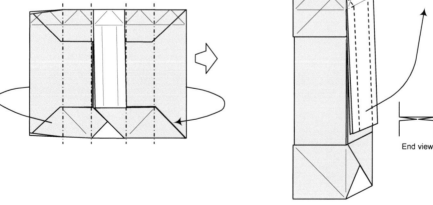

27

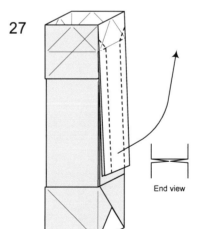

End view

Lift the flap to a horizontal position.
Shape the edges using the creases
made in steps 21 and 23.

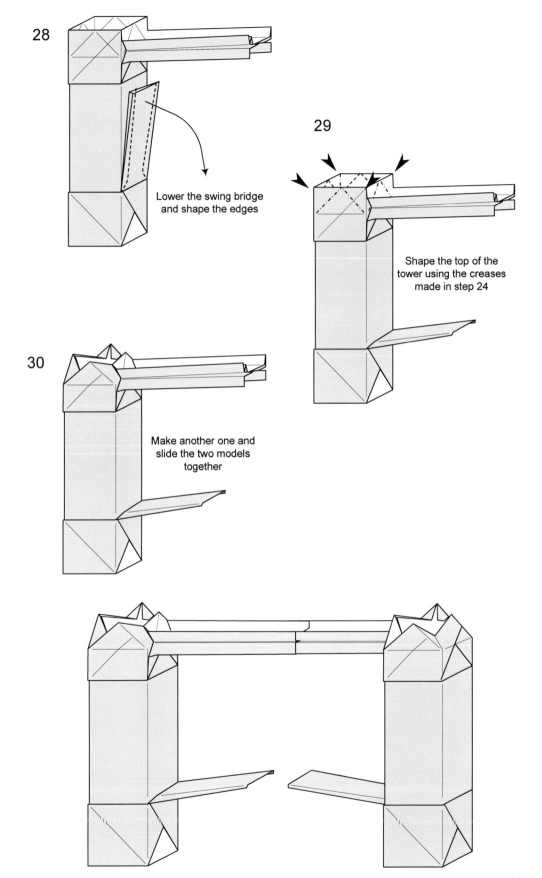

28

Lower the swing bridge
and shape the edges

29

Shape the top of the
tower using the creases
made in step 24

30

Make another one and
slide the two models
together

False Teeth

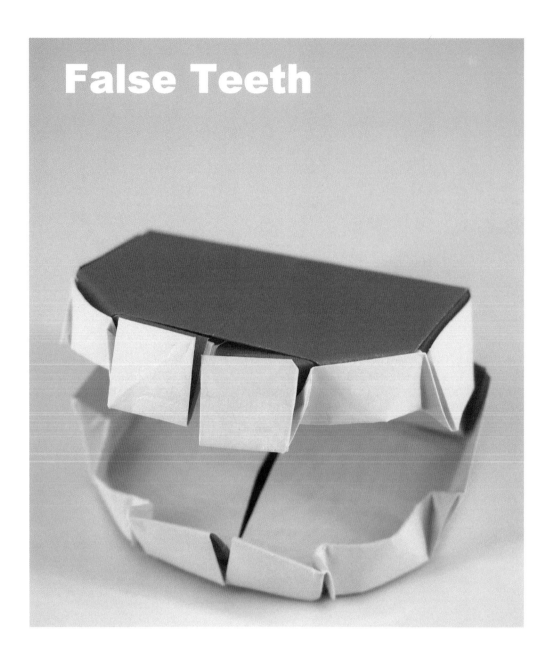

I am easily amused, and somewhat nostalgic for the toys and games I played with as a child. To be honest, I still like playing with toys. This model, designed in July 1998 was inspired by those plastic chattering teeth you find in joke shops. These false teeth do not bite with quite the same gusto as a wind-up toy, but it does have a satisfying action.

False Teeth

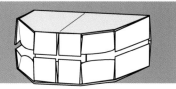

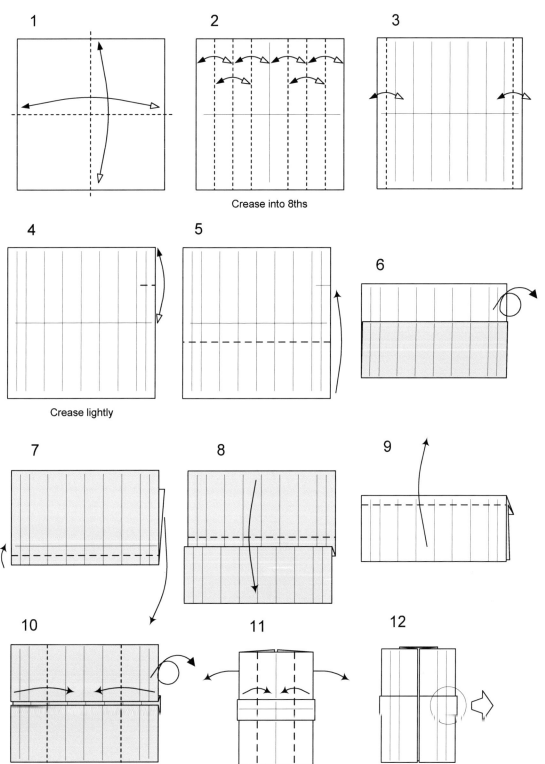

1

2

Crease into 8ths

3

4

Crease lightly

5

6

7

8

9

10

11

12

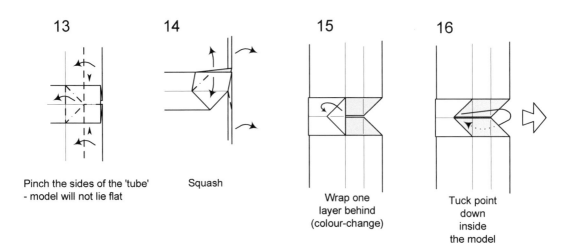

13

Pinch the sides of the 'tube'
- model will not lie flat

14

Squash

15

Wrap one
layer behind
(colour-change)

16

Tuck point
down
inside
the model

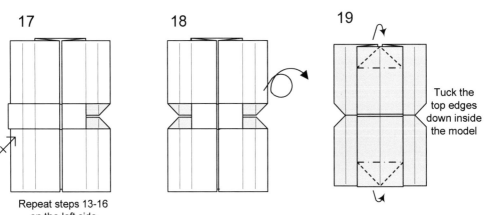

17

Repeat steps 13-16
on the left side

18

19

Tuck the
top edges
down inside
the model

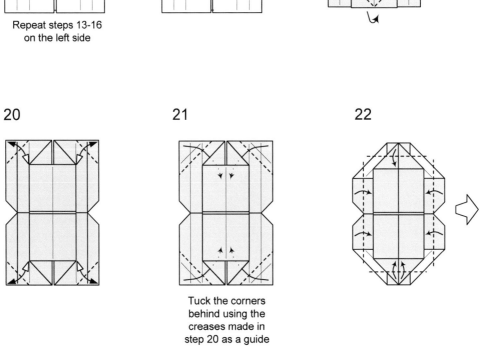

20

21

Tuck the corners
behind using the
creases made in
step 20 as a guide

22

23

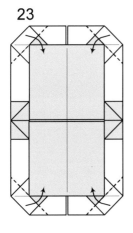

24

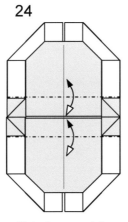

Make two mountain
creases

25

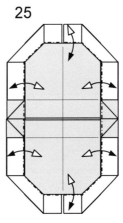

Crease more
mountain folds

26

27

Make 'teeth'
3-Dimensional
repeating on
all four corners

28

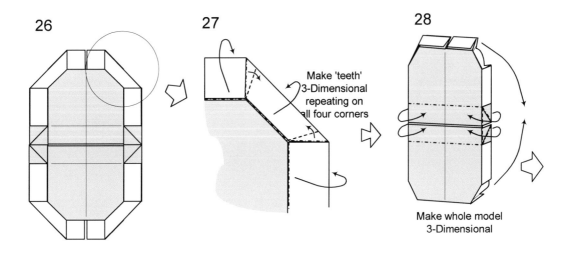

Make whole model
3-Dimensional

29

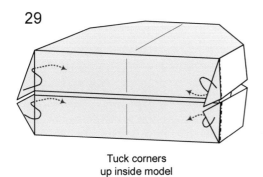

Tuck corners
up inside model

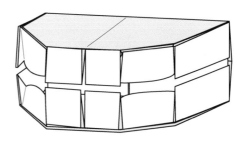

Cannon

This was designed in July 1998. A good friend of mine had the nickname
"Cannon" when we were at school. It was actually because he looked a
bit the the TV detective "Cannon" but the name stuck and I made this as
part of a Birthday gift one year. My nickname was "Vicar" for reasons too
long to explain here. I will attempt to design an origami vicar next time I
am blessed with inspiration.

Cannon

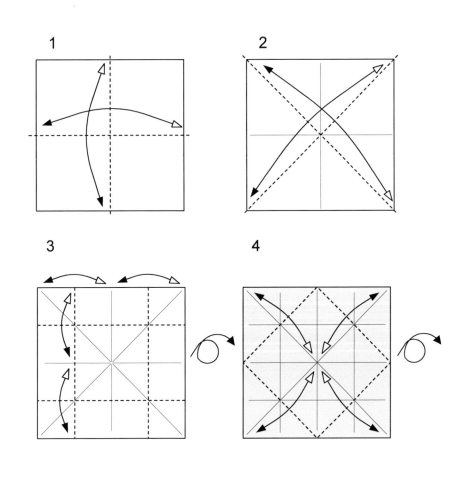

1

2

3

4

5

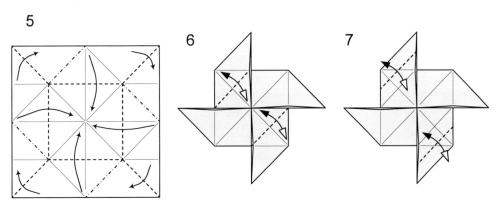

Fold a windmill base

6

7

8

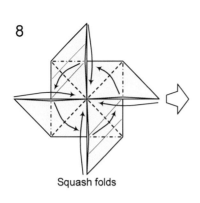

Squash folds

9

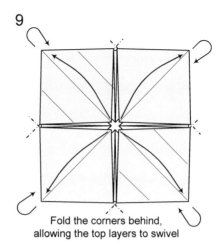

Fold the corners behind,
allowing the top layers to swivel

10

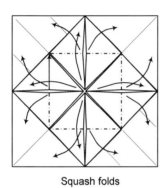

Squash folds

11

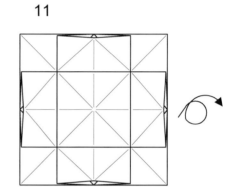

12

Pull corner

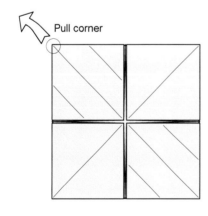

13

Stretch and collapse
on creases made in step 7

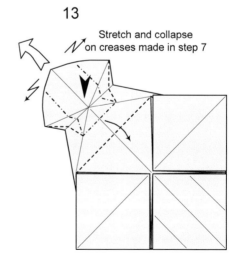

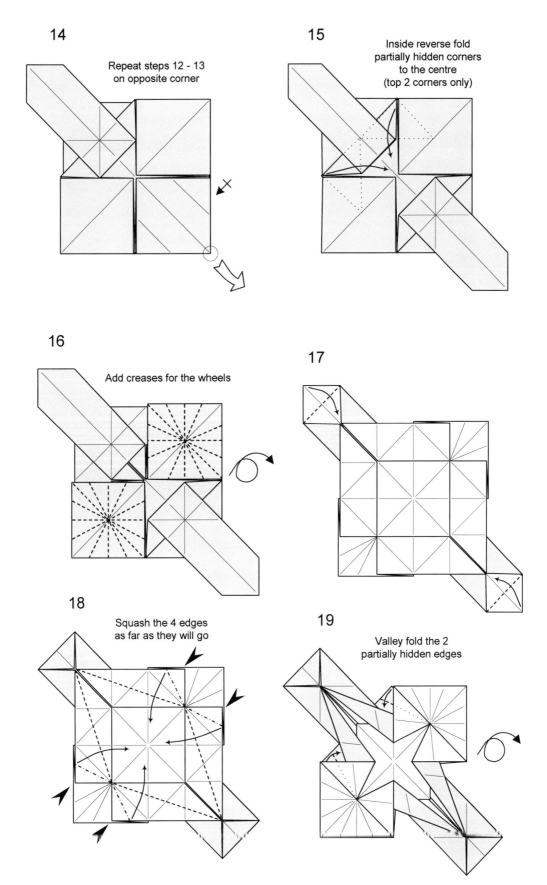

14

Repeat steps 12 - 13
on opposite corner

15

Inside reverse fold
partially hidden corners
to the centre
(top 2 corners only)

16

Add creases for the wheels

17

18

Squash the 4 edges
as far as they will go

19

Valley fold the 2
partially hidden edges

20

Mountain fold the tops of
the wheels

21

22 Make the whole model 3D
and shape the barrel to
make it round

23

Fold the tail so the
edges are vertical

24

Crimp the tail

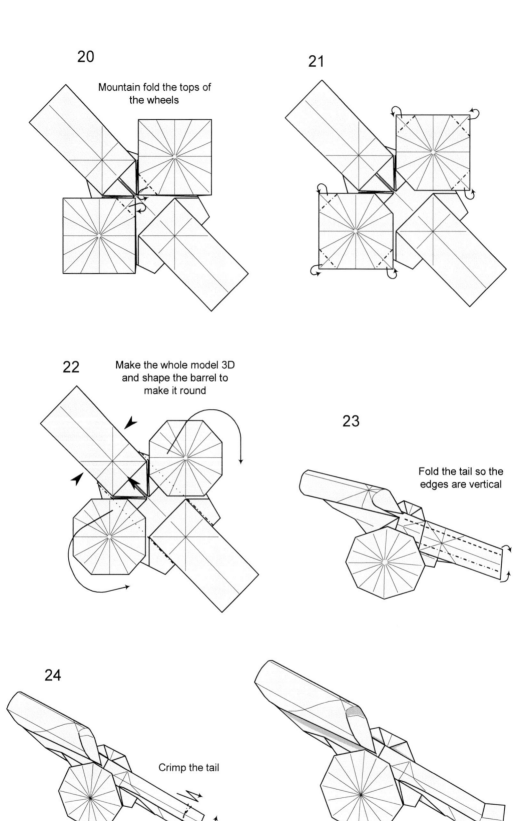

Tommy gun

I designed this model in 2005 for an origami meeting. As it was February, the theme was "Valentine's" so I tried to be original and thought of gangster movies and The St Valentine's Day Massacre. Strangely, I wasn't that original because somebody else turned up at the meeting with a similar idea! It can be folded from standard origami paper, but works best when folded at a larger scale like this one folded from a 40cm square.

Tommy gun

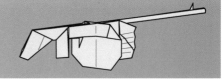

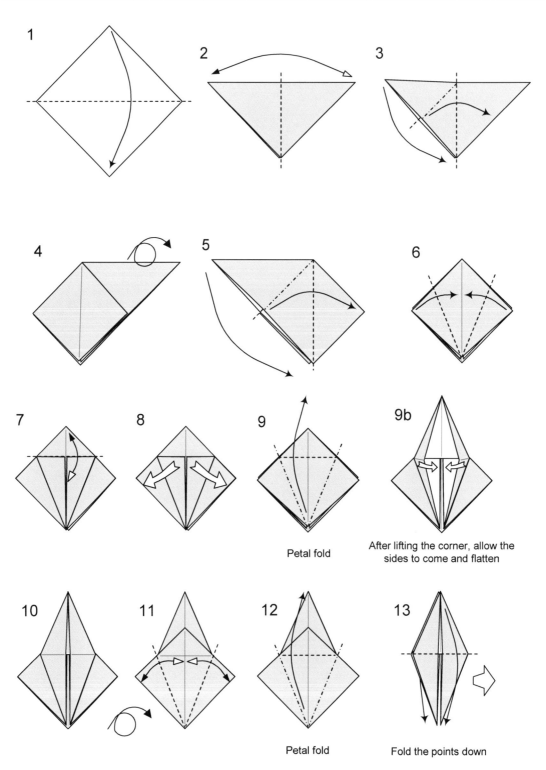

1

2

3

4

5

6

7

8

9

Petal fold

9b

After lifting the corner, allow the
sides to come and flatten

10

11

Petal fold

12

13

Fold the points down

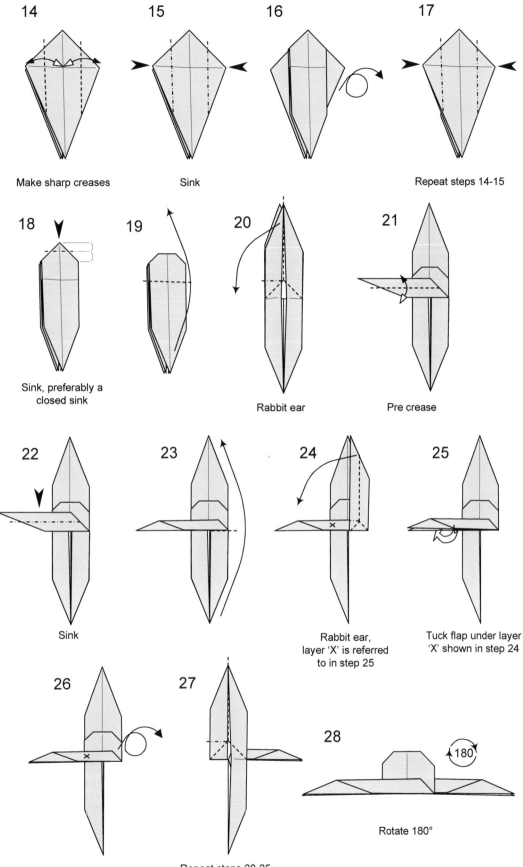

14

Make sharp creases

15

Sink

16

17

Repeat steps 14-15

18

Sink, preferably a
closed sink

19

20

Rabbit ear

21

Pre crease

22

Sink

23

24

Rabbit ear,
layer 'X' is referred
to in step 25

25

Tuck flap under layer
'X' shown in step 24

26

27

Repeat steps 20-25

28

180

Rotate 180°

29

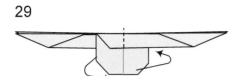

Make the model 3 dimensional

30

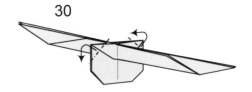

Mountain folds - the paper is quite thick!

31

Outside reverse fold the outer point only - the fold is asymmetrical

32

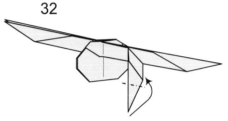

Inside reverse fold - you may have to undo step 31 slightly

33

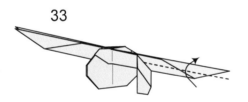

Valley fold the inner point - the fold continues all the way inside

34

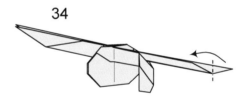

Inside reverse fold

35

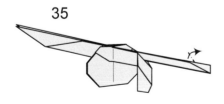

Inside reverse fold

36

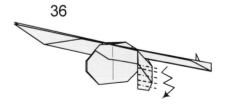

Pleat to make the 'grip'

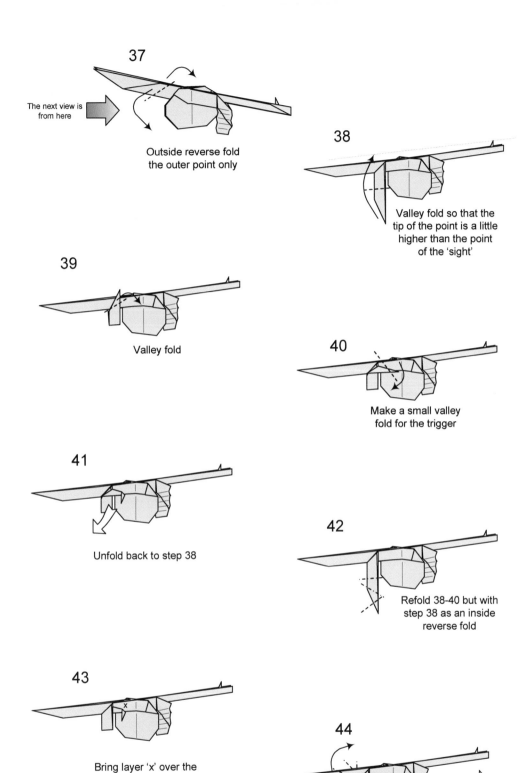

37

The next view is from here

Outside reverse fold the outer point only

38

Valley fold so that the tip of the point is a little higher than the point of the 'sight'

39

Valley fold

40

Make a small valley fold for the trigger

41

Unfold back to step 38

42

Refold 38-40 but with step 38 as an inside reverse fold

43

Bring layer 'x' over the trigger

44

Squash fold asymmetrically

45

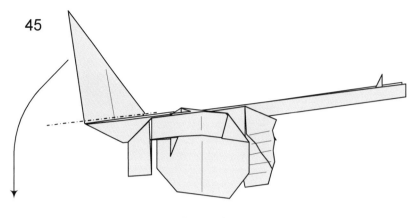

Mountain fold

46

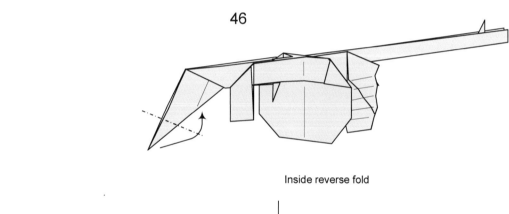

Inside reverse fold

47

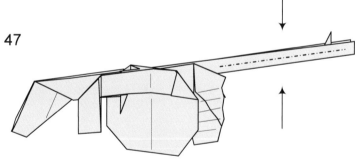

Round the barrel

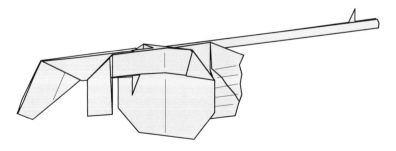

Tick-tock clock

After seeing a truly amazing origami cuckoo clock, I thought that a clock action model would be an interesting challenge. Not many origami models actually make a sound, so I had the idea of creating a clock that actually ticked. Each swing of the pendulum causes two parts of the model to brush against each other creating quite an authentic ticking sound. It is best to use fairly large paper. The model pictured here was from a trimmed down sheet of A4.

Tick-tock clock

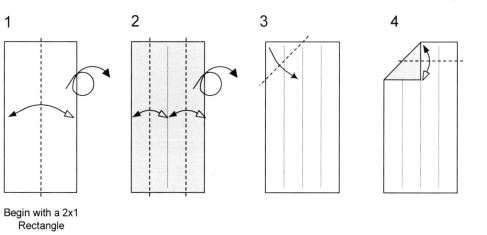

1

Begin with a 2x1 Rectangle

2

3

4

5

Unfold

6

Valley crease again

7

Valley fold at the approximate angle shown - note land mark

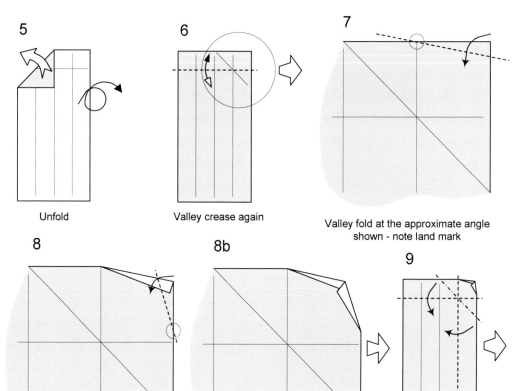

8

Valley fold the other side - make sure the crease does not start from the intersection

8b

9

Preliminary fold

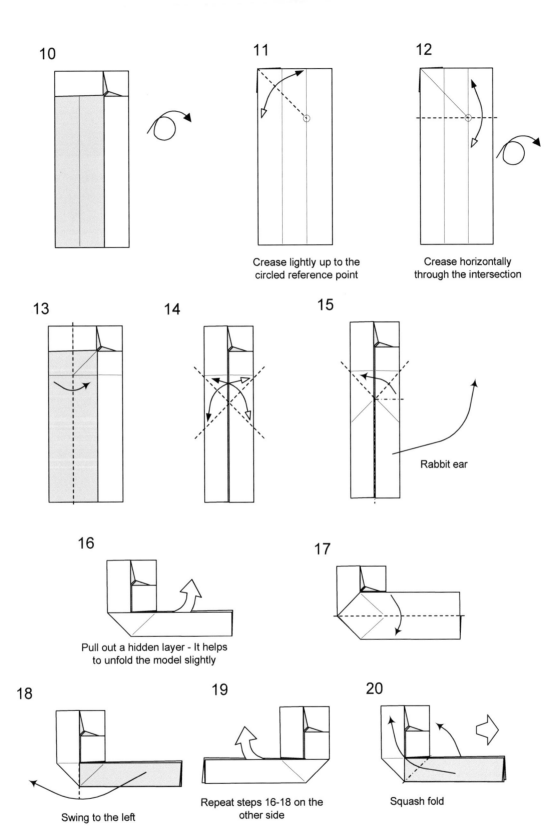

10

11

Crease lightly up to the circled reference point

12

Crease horizontally through the intersection

13

14

15

Rabbit ear

16

Pull out a hidden layer - It helps to unfold the model slightly

17

18

Swing to the left

19

Repeat steps 16-18 on the other side

20

Squash fold

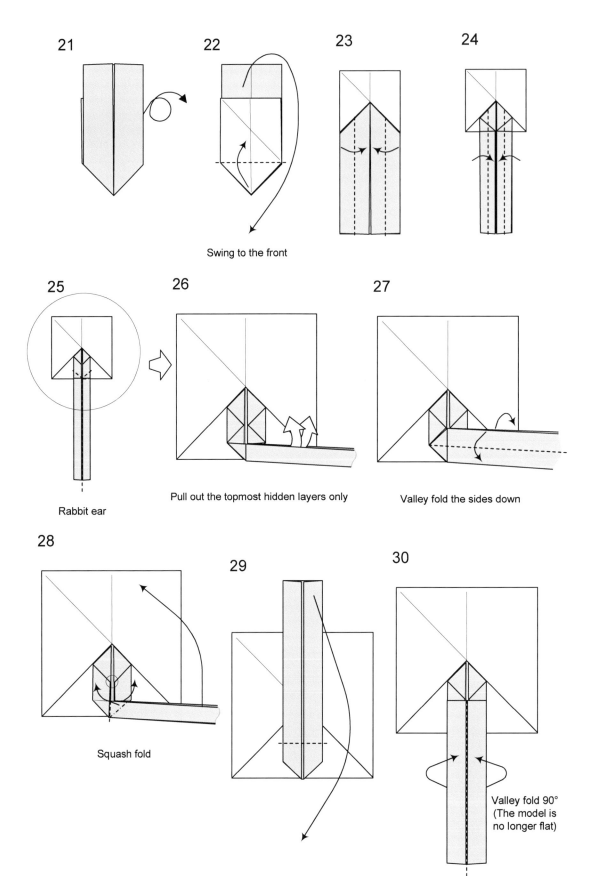

21

22

Swing to the front

23

24

25

Rabbit ear

26

Pull out the topmost hidden layers only

27

Valley fold the sides down

28

Squash fold

29

30

Valley fold 90°
(The model is
no longer flat)

31

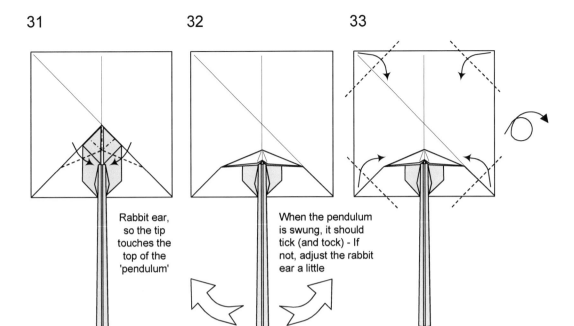

Rabbit ear,
so the tip
touches the
top of the
'pendulum'

32

When the pendulum
is swung, it should
tick (and tock) - If
not, adjust the rabbit
ear a little

33

34

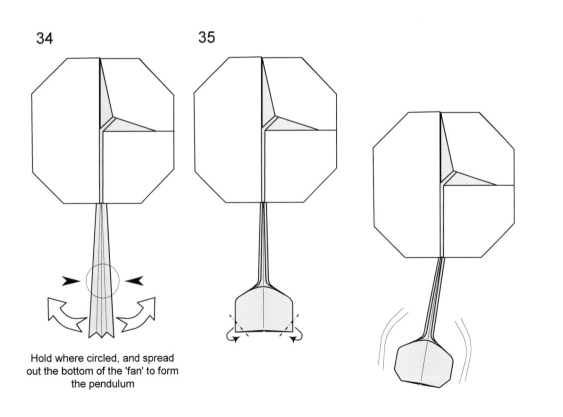

Hold where circled, and spread
out the bottom of the 'fan' to form
the pendulum

35

Submarine

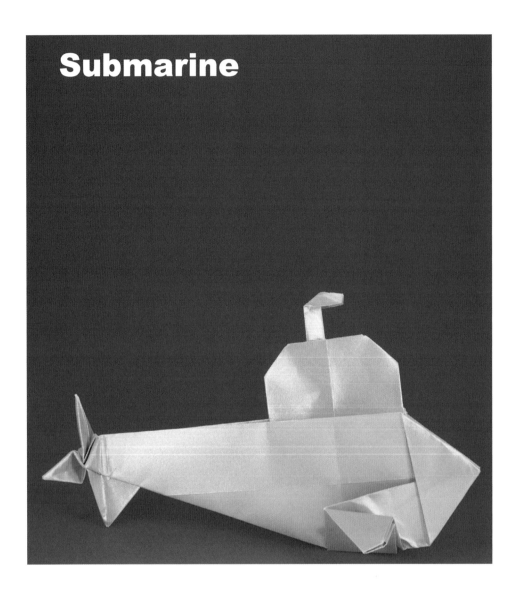

This model was originally diagrammed in June 2001. There are lots of origami vehicle models, but the submarine is a bit of a rarity. So in June 2001, I submerged myself in deep thought and this model rose from the depths of my creativity.

It has one sink fold.

Submarine

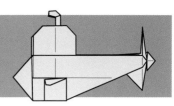

1

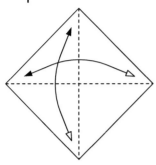

2

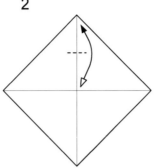

3

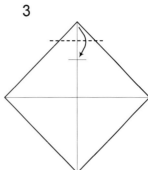

4

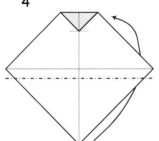

5

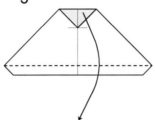

6

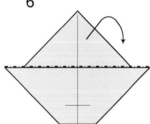

7

Fold both sides up in line
with the hidden double layer

8

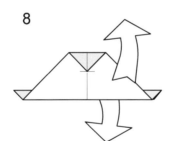

Unfold back to step 4

9

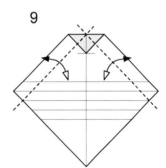

10

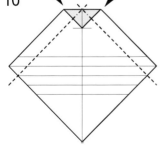

Preliminary fold

11

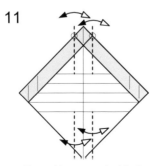

Try not to crease inside the
horizontal creases in the middle

12

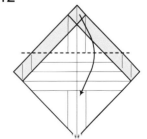

13

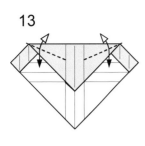

14

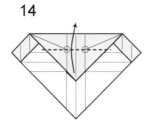

Vally fold up using the circled crease intersections as a guide

15

Squash fold using the existing creases

16

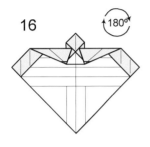

Rotate 180°

17

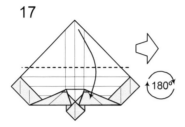

Repeat steps 12 to 16 on the other flap

18a

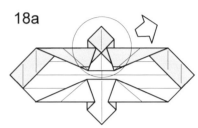

18b

Top view of layers

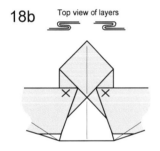

Re-fold step 15, arranging the layers so that 'X' is on the inside

18c

Top view of layers

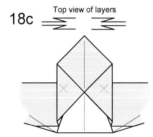

19

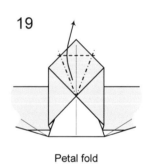

Petal fold

20

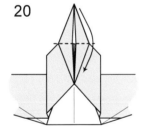

21

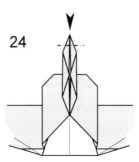

Sink

22

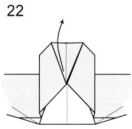

23

24

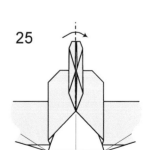

Inside reverse fold the tip

25

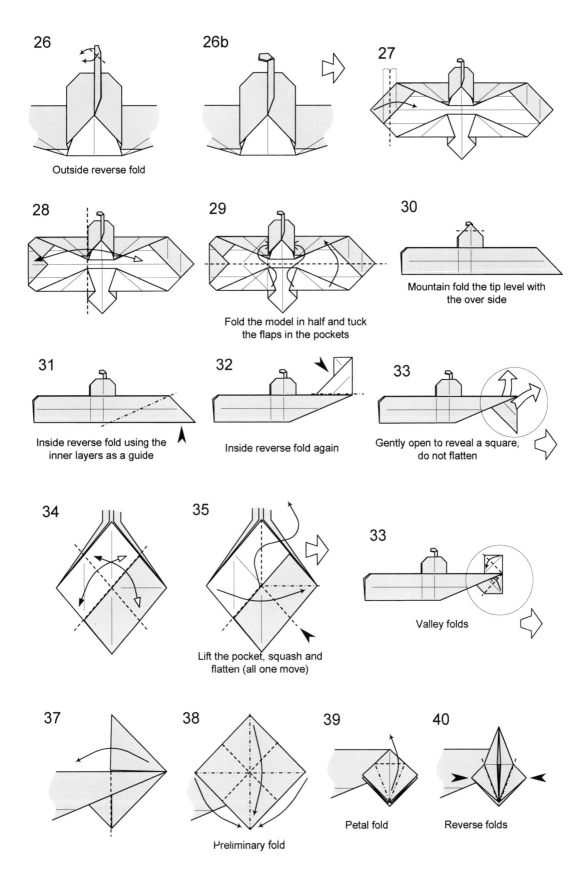

26

Outside reverse fold

26b

27

28

29

Fold the model in half and tuck
the flaps in the pockets

30

Mountain fold the tip level with
the over side

31

Inside reverse fold using the
inner layers as a guide

32

Inside reverse fold again

33

Gently open to reveal a square,
do not flatten

34

35

Lift the pocket, squash and
flatten (all one move)

33

Valley folds

37

38

Preliminary fold

39

Petal fold

40

Reverse folds

173

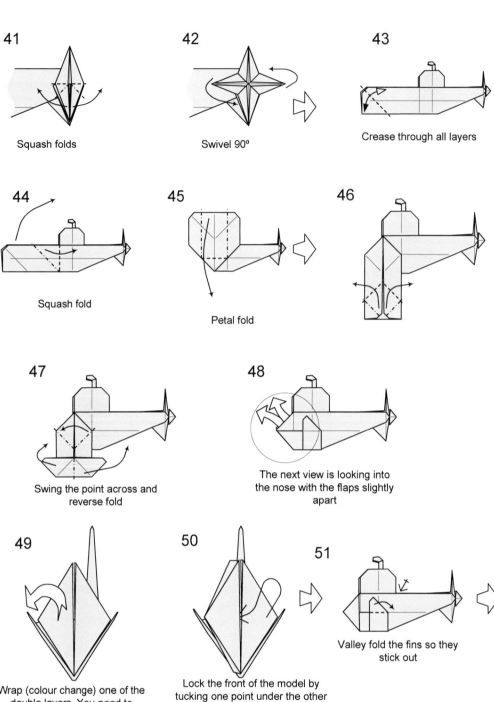

41

Squash folds

42

Swivel 90º

43

Crease through all layers

44

Squash fold

45

Petal fold

46

47

Swing the point across and reverse fold

48

The next view is looking into the nose with the flaps slightly apart

49

Wrap (colour change) one of the double layers. You need to unfold the paper a little to do this

50

Lock the front of the model by tucking one point under the other (unfold a bit to make it easier)

51

Valley fold the fins so they stick out

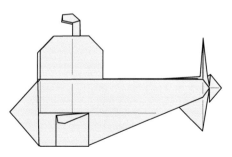

Yacht

Designed in May 2001, the yacht is intended to look like a child's drawing of a boat. In order to get a narrow mast, the design had to be quite complex. The neat thing is that all the complexity is hidden inside the model.

I thought it would be fun to make the mast half as thin again. The same principle is used, but it it much harder to fold. These were folded using 21cm Kraft paper. It also works well with smaller paper.

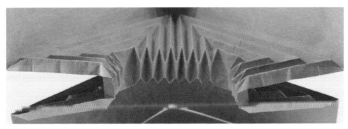

Details of the interior of the extra-thin version

Yacht

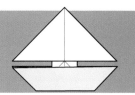

1

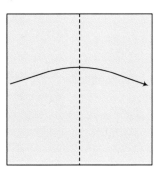

Fold in half

2

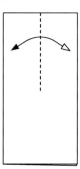

Crease through both layers, but only on the top half of the paper

3

4

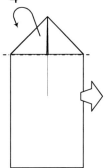

5

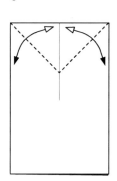

6

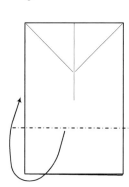

Mountain fold behind - see the next diagram for how to judge where the fold needs to be

7

This gap is twice the height of the mast

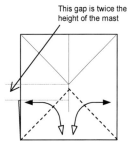

Crease the diagonals to the centre. Only crease through the top 2 layers

8

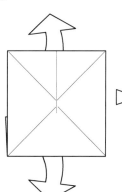

Unfold the top and bottom

9

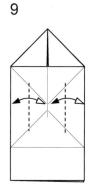

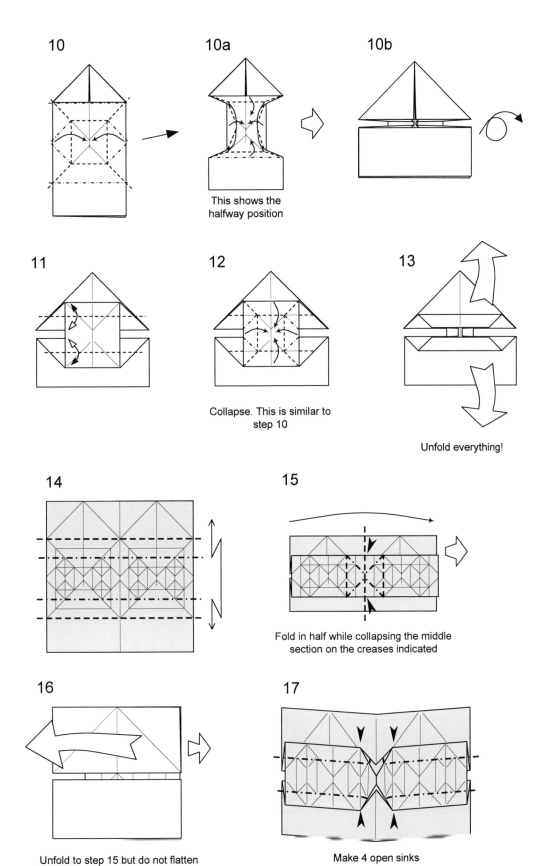

10

10a

This shows the
halfway position

10b

11

12

Collapse. This is similar to
step 10

13

Unfold everything!

14

15

Fold in half while collapsing the middle
section on the creases indicated

16

Unfold to step 15 but do not flatten

17

Make 4 open sinks

18

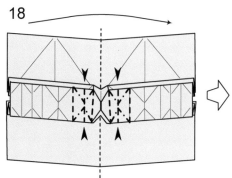

Fold in half while collapsing the 2
sections (just like in step 15)

19

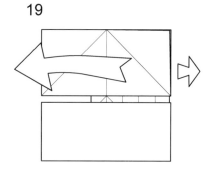

Unfold again, but do not flatten

20

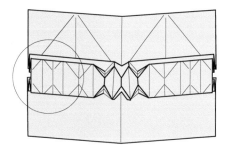

For the next few steps only the circled
area is shown

21

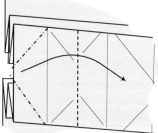

Fold and stretch

22

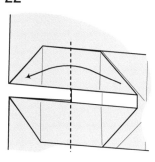

Valley fold

23

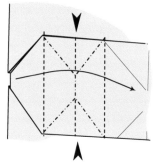

Fold back again while collapsing
on the existing creases

24

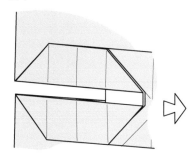

25

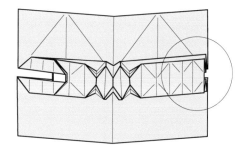

Repeat steps 21-23 on the other side

26

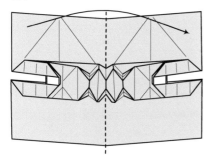

Fold in half and flatten

27

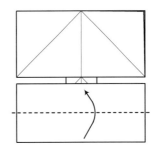

Valley fold both layers up

28

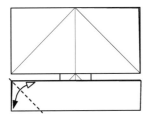

Crease through all layers

29

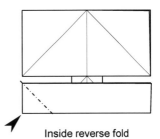

Inside reverse fold

30

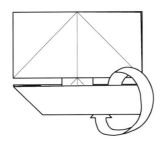

Wrap a single layer behind. To do
this easily, you need to unfold the
model slightly

31

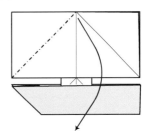

Squash fold

32

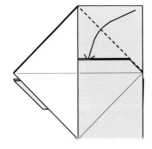

Valley fold and tuck behind
all the other layers

33

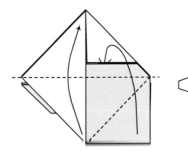

Valley fold the corner and tuck
behind to lock

34

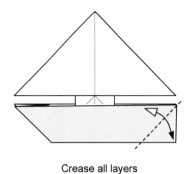

Crease all layers

35

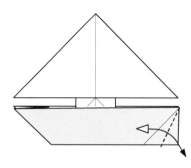

36

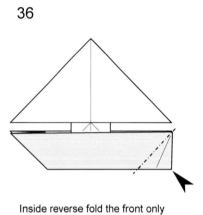

Inside reverse fold the front only

37

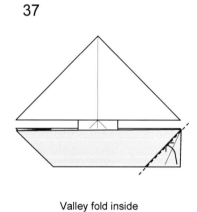

Valley fold inside

38

It's not essential, but there is a
hidden flap inside this sail which
can be locked the same way

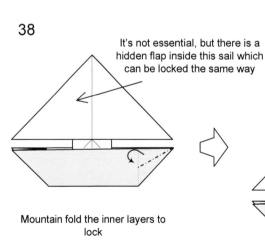

Mountain fold the inner layers to
lock

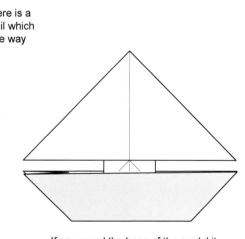

If you round the base of the model it
will stand up

Eiffel Tower

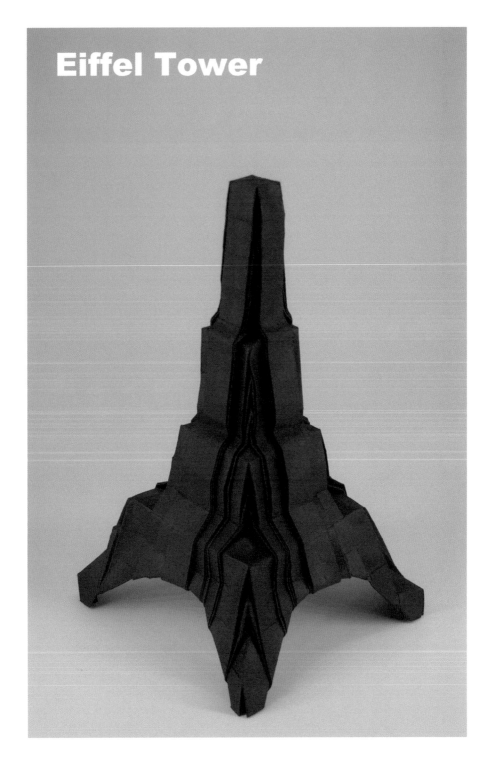

The Eiffel Tower model was designed in December 1999. It is a time-consuming model to make - this one, folded from a square made from A2 paper, took me four hours to fold. I have made one from standard 15cm origami paper, but I am not sure my eyes are good enough to do that now.

Eiffel Tower

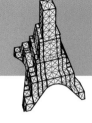

1

Begin with a square, white side up creased into a 32 by 32 grid of valley folds. Trim one square from the top and side to make a 31 by 31 grid.

2

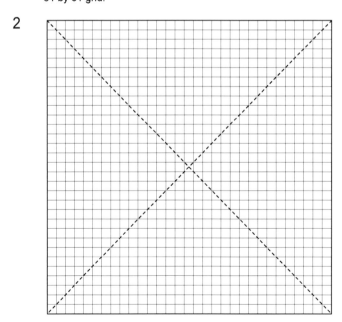

Crease the diagonals, if you feel up to it, crease every diagonal to make the 'girders'. For clarity, the extra diagonals are not shown on the remaining diagrams.

3

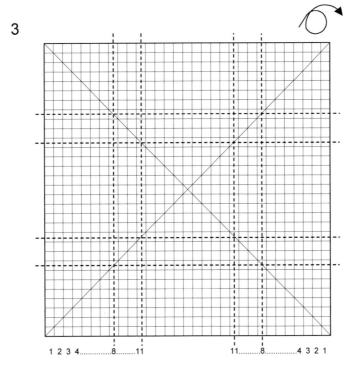

1 2 3 4.............8........11   11.........8.............4 3 2 1

Bisect the 11th and 8th sements from the edge of each side

4

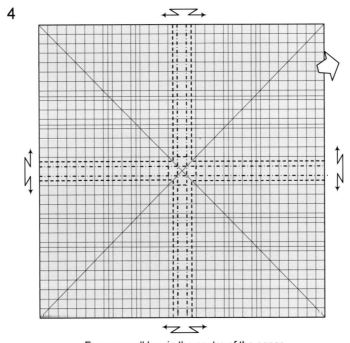

Form a small box in the centre of the paper

5

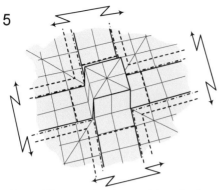

Repeat the procedure in step 4 to make the
box taller

6

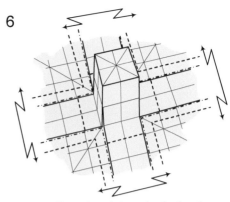

Repeat again to make the box 3
segments tall

7

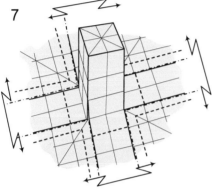

Repeat one more time to make
the box 4 segments tall

8

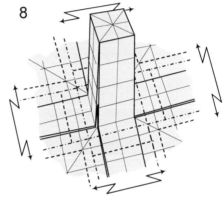

Starting on the half segment crease, make another stack
3 segments tall. I usually pre-crease all 3 segments and
form the stack in one (slightly tricky) move.

9

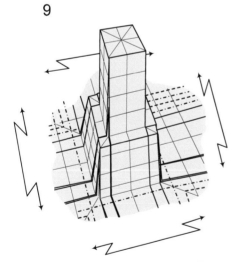

Make the next stack 2 segments tall

10

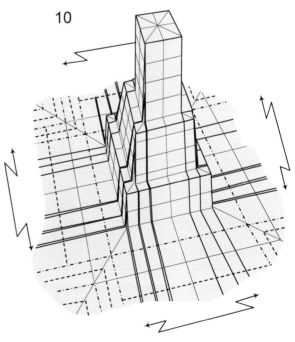

Make another 2 segment stack

11

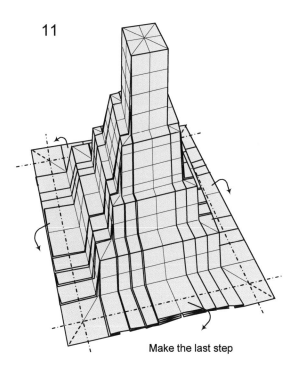

Make the last step

12

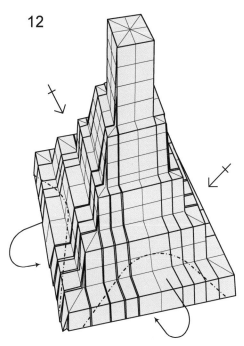

Mountain fold an arc shaped crease up inside
the model, allowing the multiple thicknesses
to fan out slightly.

13

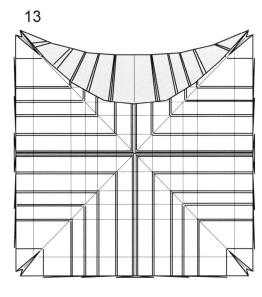

View from underside showing a 'fanned' edge

14

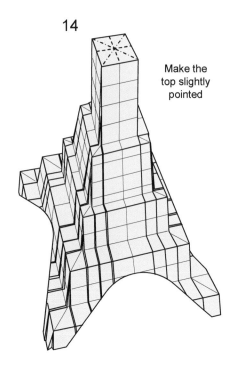

Make the
top slightly
pointed

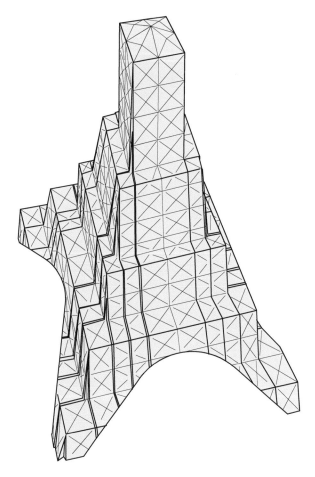

Heart Badge

This badge was designed in October 2017. It is a very simple design and has a neat way of locking that works like a safety pin.

Heart Badge

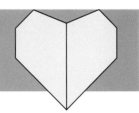

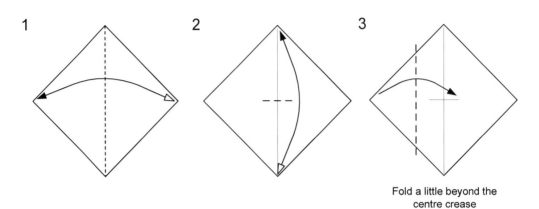

3

Fold a little beyond the
centre crease

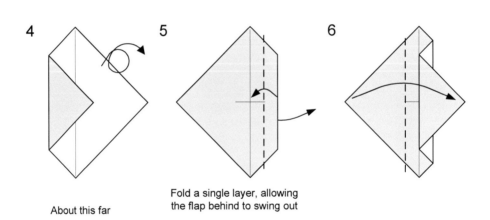

4

About this far

5

Fold a single layer, allowing
the flap behind to swing out

6

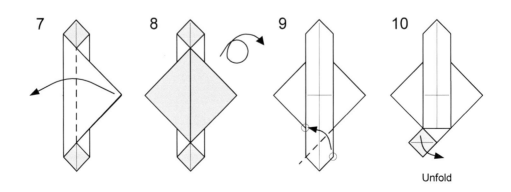

9

10

Unfold

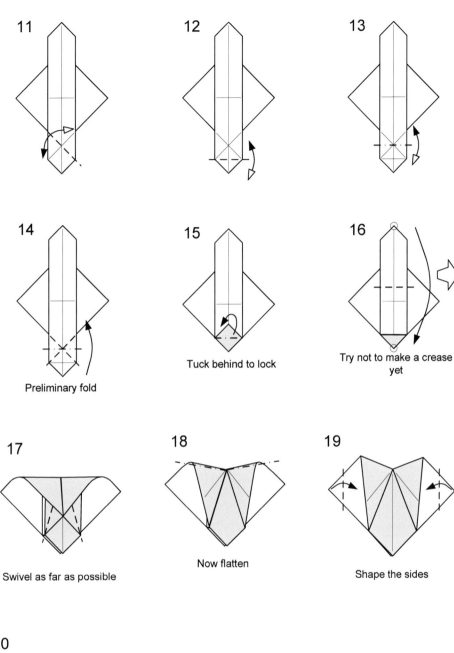

11

12

13

14

Preliminary fold

15

Tuck behind to lock

16

Try not to make a crease yet

17

Swivel as far as possible

18

Now flatten

19

Shape the sides

20

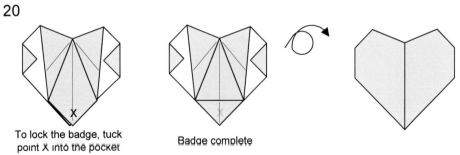

To lock the badge, tuck point X into the pocket

Badge complete

8 Pointed Star

This was designed in October 2017. It is very simple to fold and assemble. It also lends itself to variations. By changing step 5 from a valley fold to a mountain fold, we get the variation shown below...

8 Pointed Star

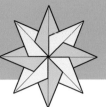

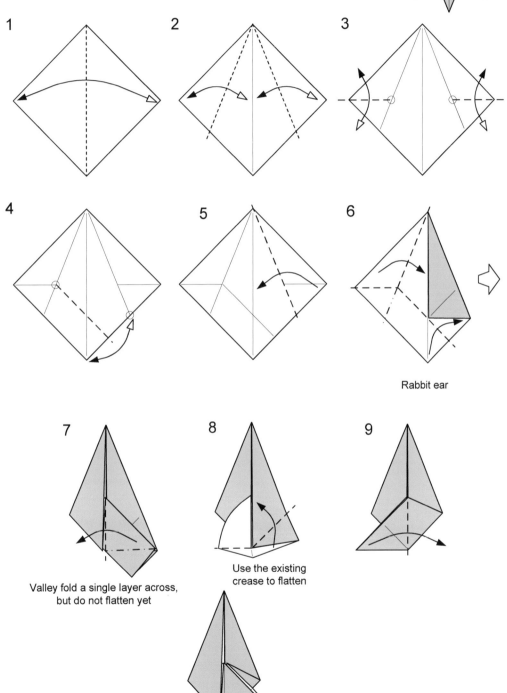

1

2

3

4

5

6

Rabbit ear

7

Valley fold a single layer across,
but do not flatten yet

8

Use the existing
crease to flatten

9

Finished unit, make 7 more

Assembly

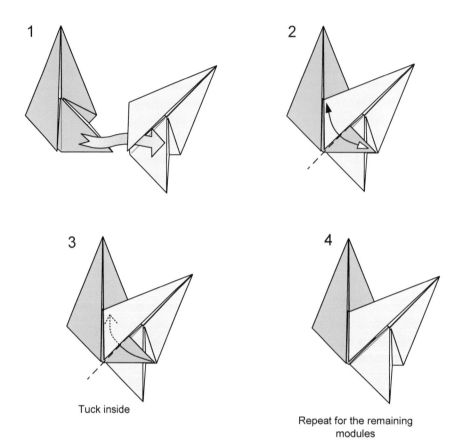

1

2

3

Tuck inside

4

Repeat for the remaining
modules

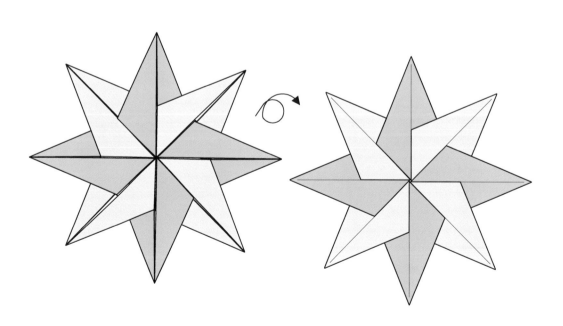

6 Pointed modular star

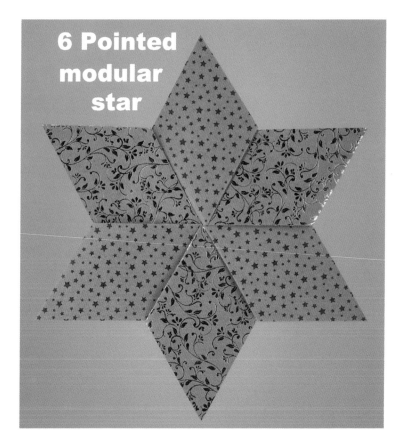

This was my first modular star. It was designed it in October 2017 when my partner was looking for elements to use for her card making.

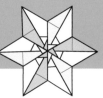

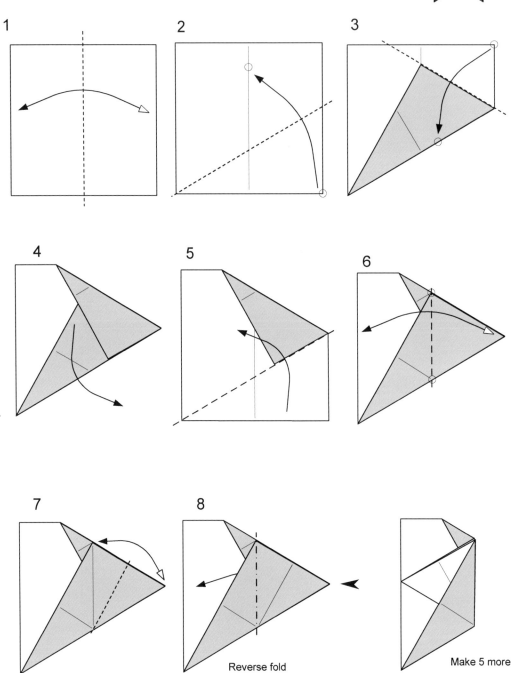

1

2

3

4

5

6

7

8

Reverse fold

Make 5 more

Assembly

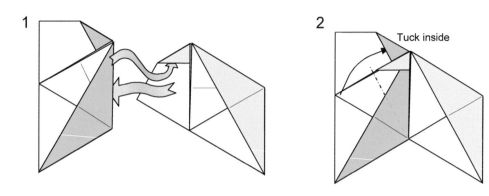

1

2 Tuck inside

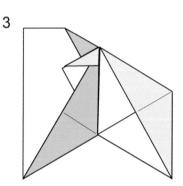

3

Repeat for the remaining 4
modules

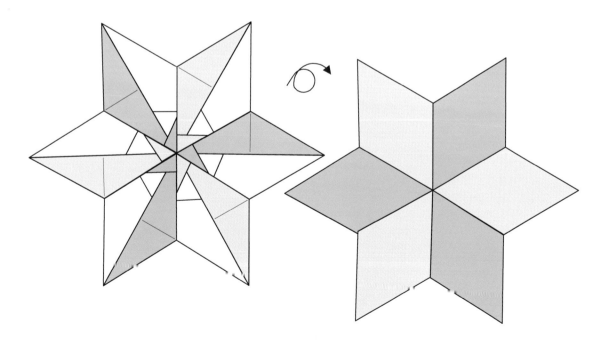

12 Pointed star ring

This star was created in October 2017. After designing a 6 pointed star, a 12 pointed version was a natural progression. The model pictured here was folded using 10cm squares coloured the same on both sides. It works really well with most sizes and thicknesses of paper.

12 Pointed star ring

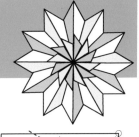

1

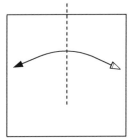

Try not to crease the all the way to the bottom edge

2

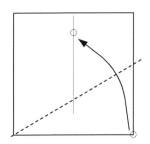

3

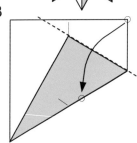

4

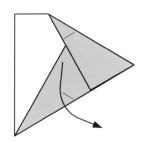

5

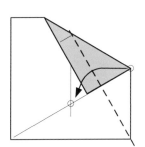

6

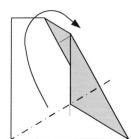

7

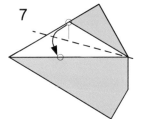

8

It's best to fold a little short of this edge

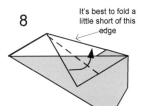

9

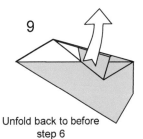

Unfold back to before step 6

10

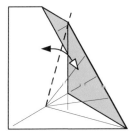

Refold crease as a valley fold

11

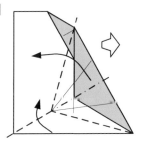

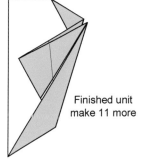

Finished unit make 11 more

Assembly

1

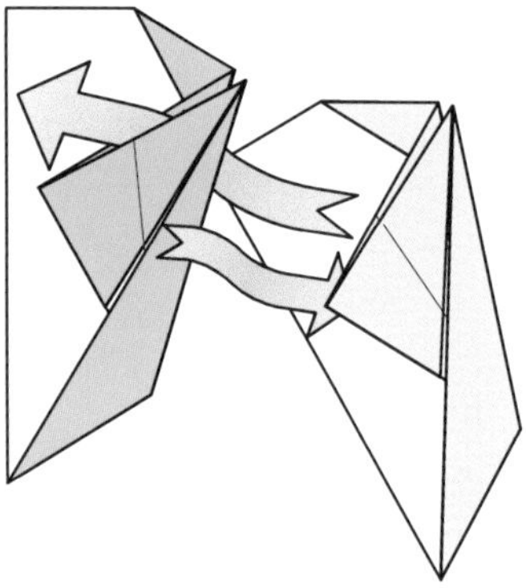

2

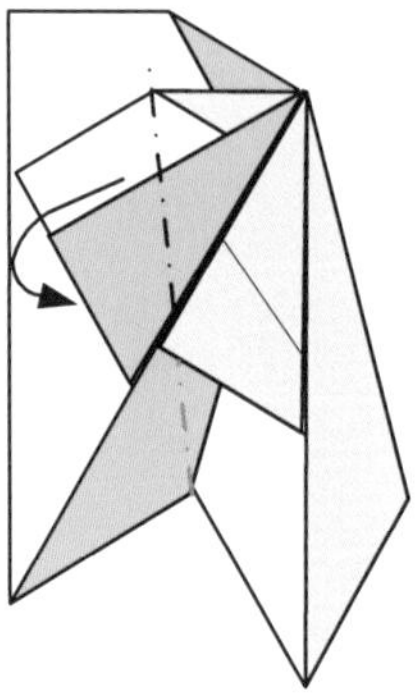

Mountain fold behind

3

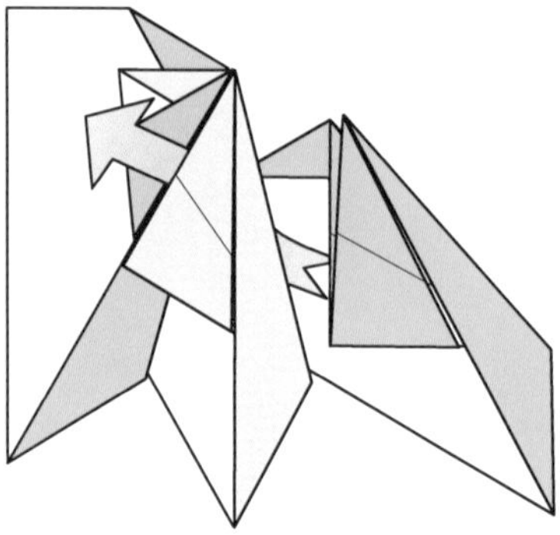

Slide in another unit

4

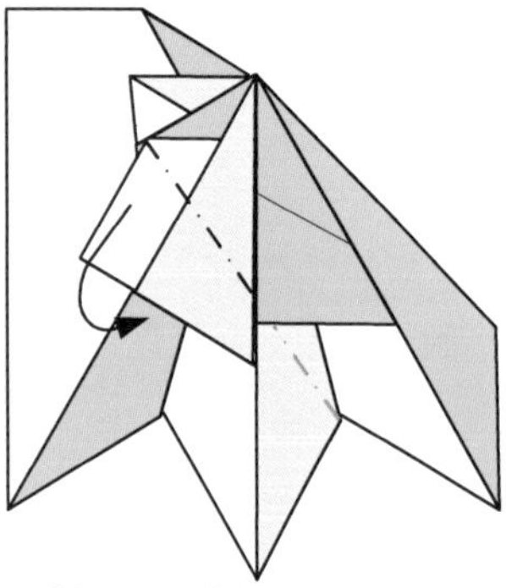

Mountain fold behind

5

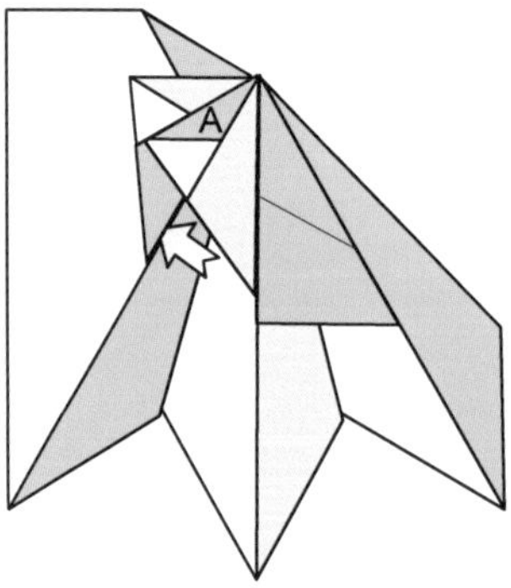

Tuck flap A into the pocket

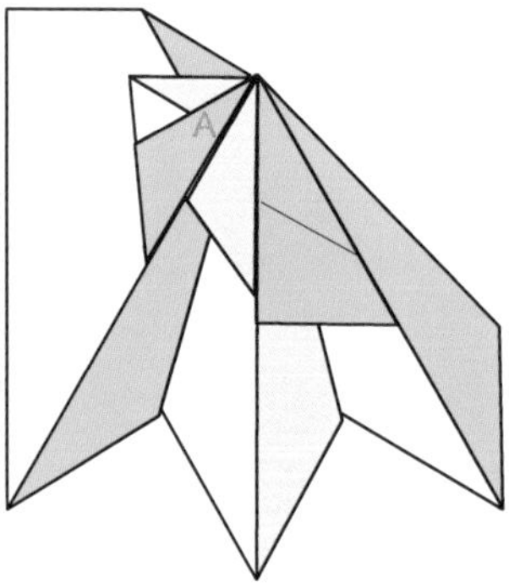

Add the remaining units the same way

8 Pointed Woven Stars

This model was designed at the same time as the 6 pointed woven stars. This is a nice model and it holds together well, but I think I prefer the 6 pointed version. Not least because folding 16 identical units can be a little tedious. One remedy for this is to play loud music while folding.

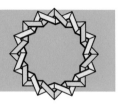

We need 16 2x1 rectangles, here we have
2 differently coloured squares

1

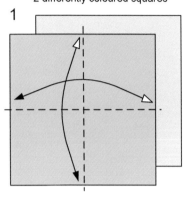

2

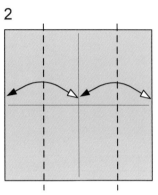

3

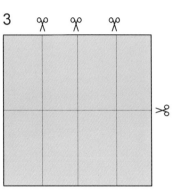

Cut into 8 2x1 rectangles

1

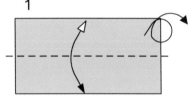

2

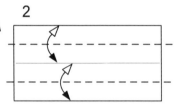

3

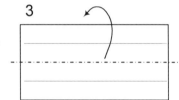

4

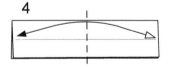

5

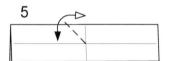

6

7

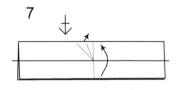

8

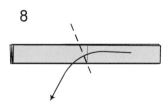

Use hidden crease from step 6

9

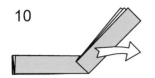

10

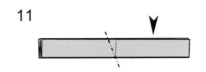

11

Inside reverse fold

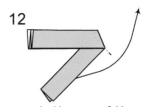

12

Inside reverse fold

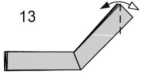

13

Only crease the first 2 layers

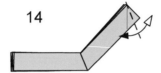

14

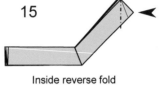

15

Inside reverse fold

16

17

Repeat steps 13-15

Unit complete - make 15 more

Assembly

1

The corner tucks behind the
point, the same thing happens
at the back

2

To lock, mountain fold the inner
corners using the creases made
in step 14

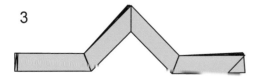

3

Add 6 more units to finish one star

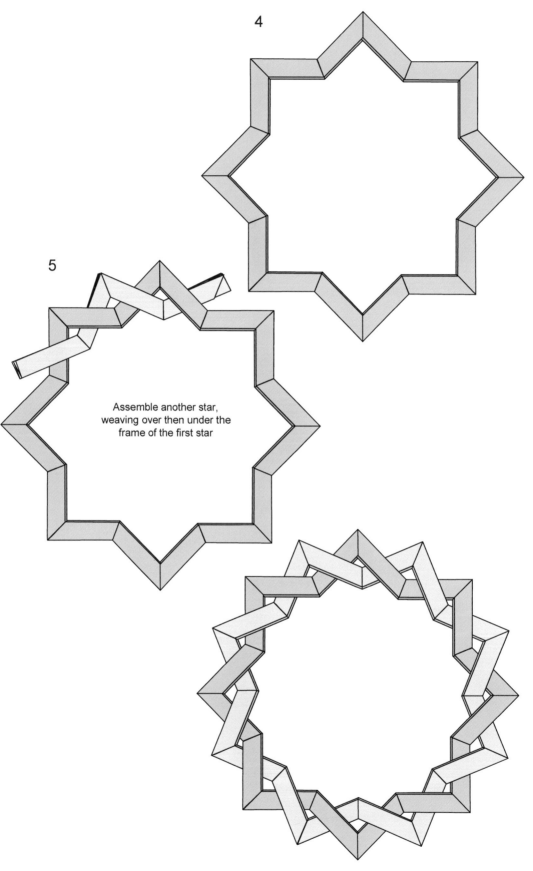

4

5

Assemble another star,
weaving over then under the
frame of the first star

6 Pointed Woven Stars

This model was designed in November 2017. It was one of those times when the idea suddenly came to me when I wasn't even thinking about origami. Aside from a few minor adjustments, the woven stars went from idea to completed model in less than an hour. To be honest, it is more satisfying if the journey from idea to finished product is a long and tortuous road. The model is enjoyable to fold and comes out fine with just about any type and size of paper.

6 Pointed Woven Stars

1

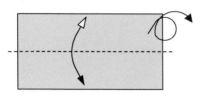

You will need 12 2x1 rectangles, preferably 6 each of two colours

2

3

4

5

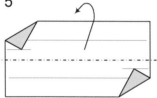

6

7

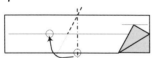

Only crease the diagonal as far as the centre line

8

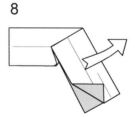

9

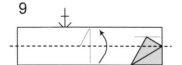

Fold up, repeat behind

10

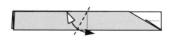

Using the crease from step 7, crease through all the layers

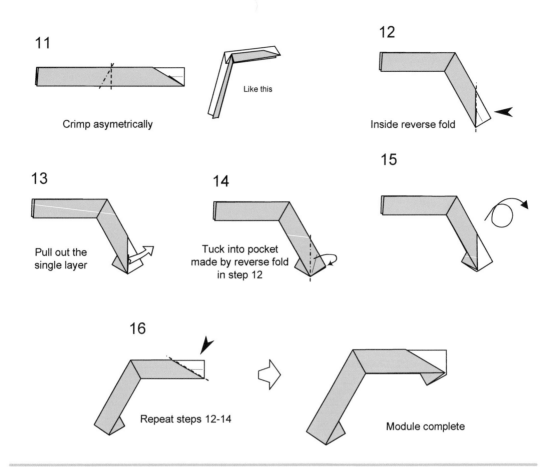

11

Crimp asymetrically

Like this

12

Inside reverse fold

13

Pull out the
single layer

14

Tuck into pocket
made by reverse fold
in step 12

15

16

Repeat steps 12-14

Module complete

Assembly

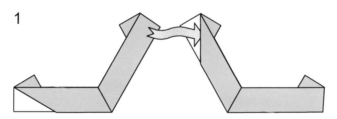

1

Slide the tab into the pocket, doing the
same to the back

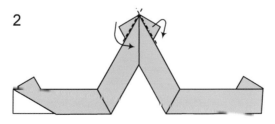

2

Valley one flap to the front, and the
other behind

3

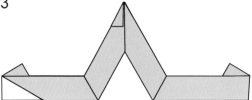

Tuck the flaps inside

4

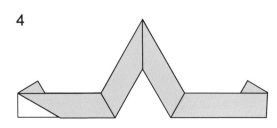

Add 4 more units the same way to
complete one star

5

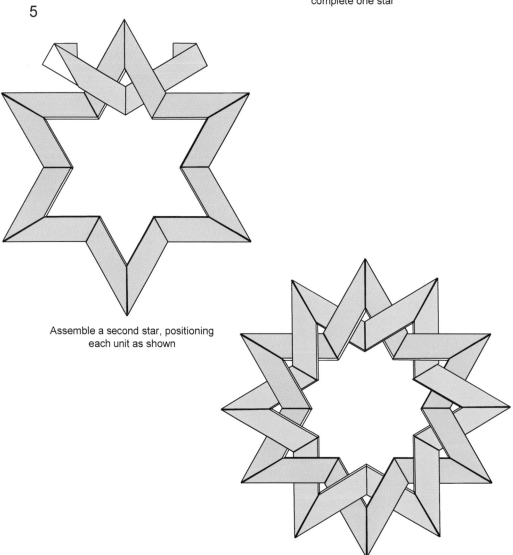

Assemble a second star, positioning
each unit as shown

Braided Bird Star

I designed this in November 2017. After working on a couple of modular stars, I looked around to see what other designers had created. I discovered the fantastic work of Maria Sinayskaya. I particularly liked a model of hers called the "Braided Corona Star". I liked the idea of braiding so set myself the challenge of creating a star that was braided on both sides. After a little experimentation, I found this novel use for a bird base.

Braided Bird Star

1

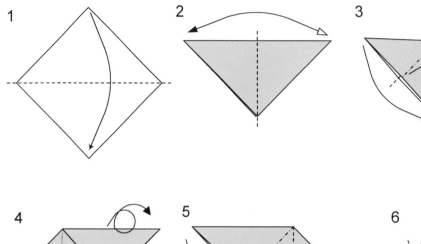

2

3

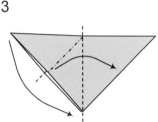

4

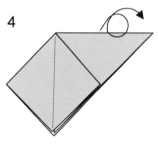

5

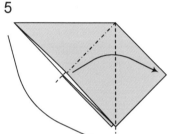

6

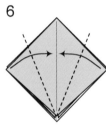

7

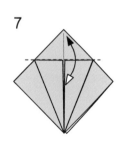

8

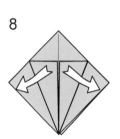

9

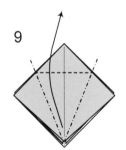

Petal fold

9b

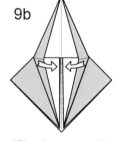

After lifting the corner, allow the
sides to come together

10

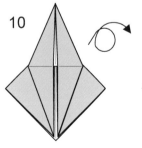

11

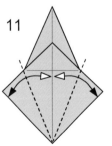

Petal fold

12

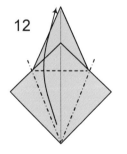

13

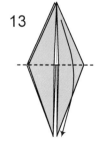

This is a bird base

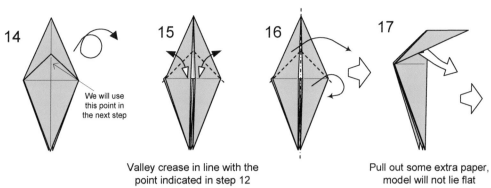

14

We will use this point in the next step

15

Valley crease in line with the point indicated in step 12

16

17

Pull out some extra paper, model will not lie flat

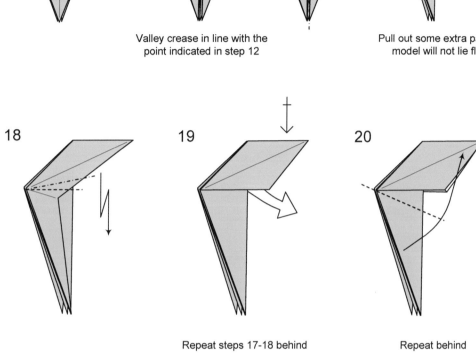

18

19

Repeat steps 17-18 behind

20

Repeat behind

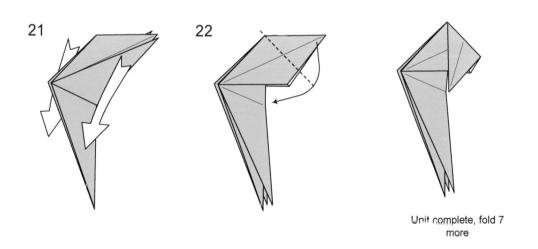

21

22

Unit complete, fold 7 more

Assembly

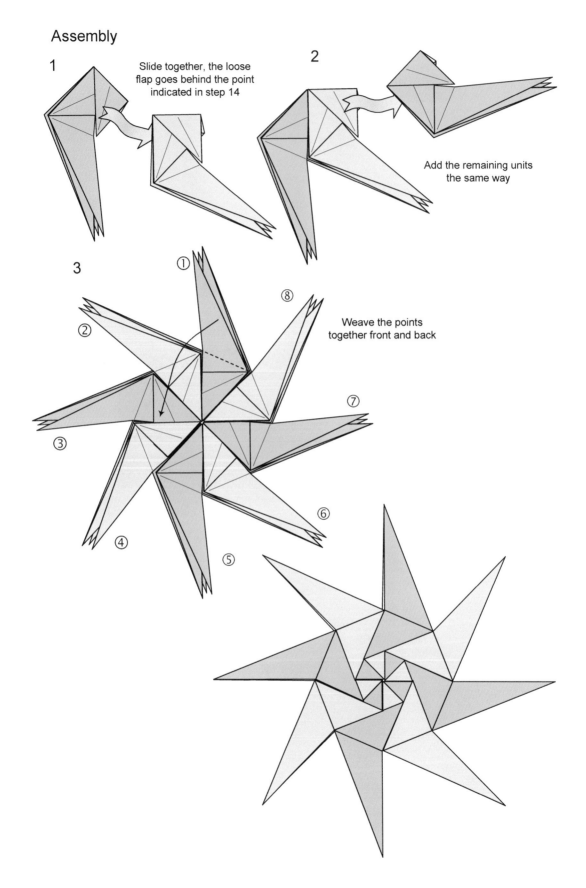

1

Slide together, the loose flap goes behind the point indicated in step 14

2

Add the remaining units the same way

3

① ② ③ ④ ⑤ ⑥ ⑦ ⑧

Weave the points together front and back

Xmas Tree Box Decoration

In October 2017, I was experimenting with quite elaborate box designs where the top of the box had a specific shape. The models were far too complicated to be folded neatly, so I decided to make a separate model that would attach to a box. My first design was a heart shape which is also included in this book. This was my second idea. There is lots of scope for further "box toppers". I have for instance, folded a version of the grim reaper that makes a good Halloween themed box.

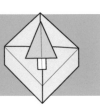

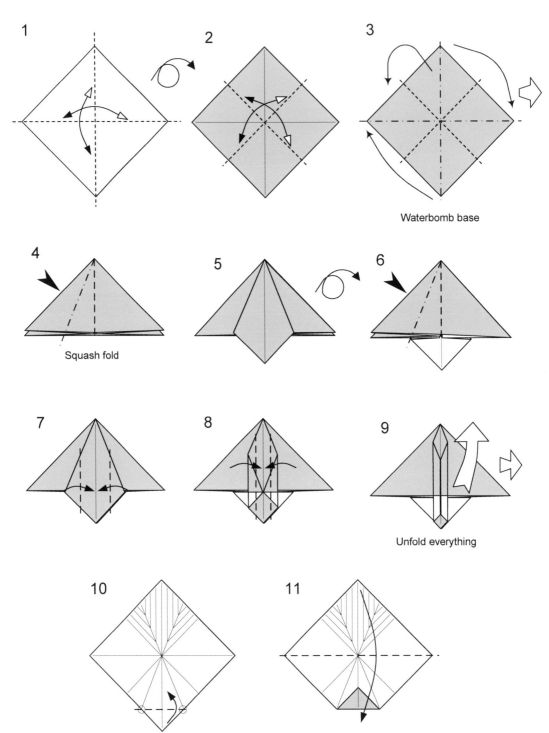

1

2

3

Waterbomb base

4

Squash fold

5

6

7

8

9

Unfold everything

10

11

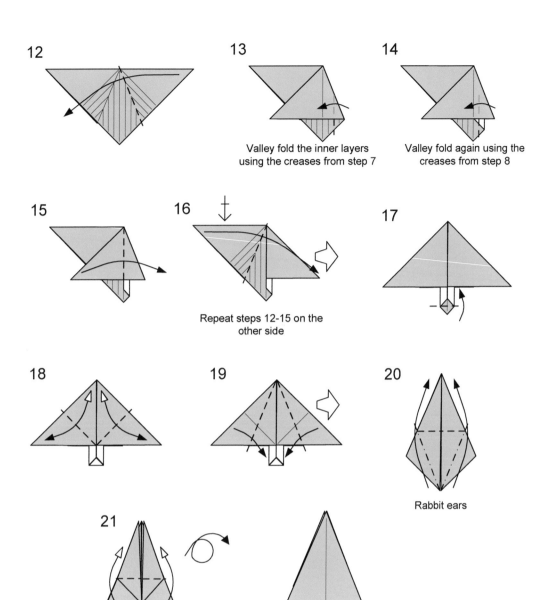

12

13

Valley fold the inner layers
using the creases from step 7

14

Valley fold again using the
creases from step 8

15

16

Repeat steps 12-15 on the
other side

17

18

19

20

Rabbit ears

21

These points are used
to insert into a box
(one folds down)

Finished model

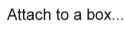
Attach to a box...

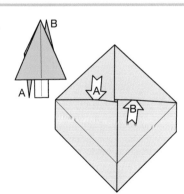

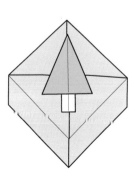

Heart Box Decoration

I designed this in October 2017. Originally, I had the idea of a box where the four flaps of the lid came together to form a heart shape. All my efforts turned out far too complicated for my satisfaction. Then I had the idea of creating a heart shaped model with tabs that could slot into a box. This was a far more elegant solution. That does not mean that I have completely given up with my original plan.

Heart Box Decoration

1

2

3

Preliminary fold

4

Squash fold

5

6

Squash fold

7

Unfold everything

8

9

Crimp using the existing creases

10

Valley fold down - this will raise some hidden paper - do not flatten yet

11

Flatten with a squash fold

12

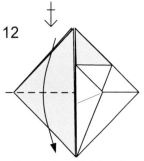

Repeat steps 10-11 on the other side

13

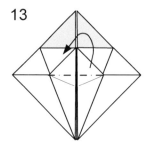

Mountain fold behind

14

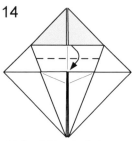

Valley fold a single layer, but do not flatten

15

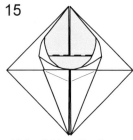

Valley fold another layer, but do not flatten

16

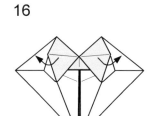

Squash flat so the corners lie along the raw edges

17

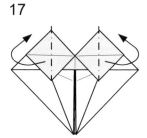

Mountain fold behind - it is easier to valley fold first

18

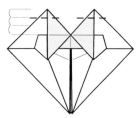

Fold the tips down by approximately a third

19

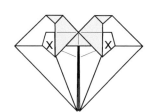

Re-arrange the layers so the indicated points are inside

20

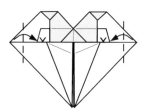

21

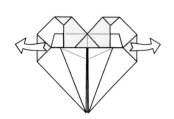

22

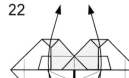

23

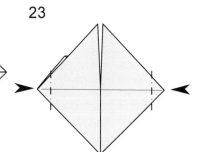

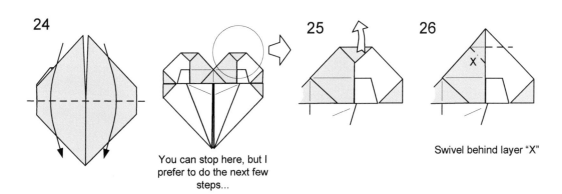

24

25

26

You can stop here, but I prefer to do the next few steps...

Swivel behind layer "X"

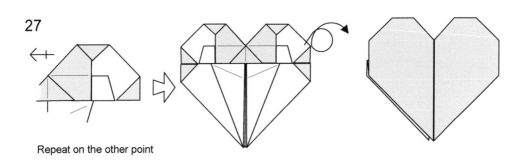

27

Repeat on the other point

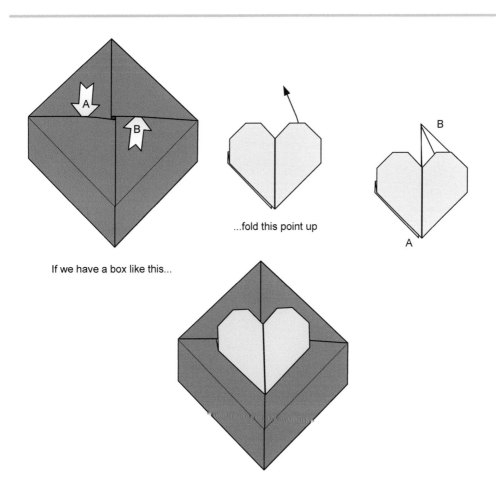

If we have a box like this...

...fold this point up

Printed in Great Britain
by Amazon

48945471R00126